HANDFUL OF KEYS

HANDFUL OF KEYS

CONVERSATIONS WITH THIRTY JAZZ PIANISTS

ALYN SHIPTON

ROUTLEDGE

NEW YORK

First Published 2004
by Equinox Publishing Ltd.
Unit 6, The Village, 101 Amies St., London, SW11 2JW

www.equinoxpub.com

Simultaneously published in the USA and Canada
by Routledge
270 Madison Avenue, New York, NY 10016

Routledge is an imprint of the Taylor & Francis Group

© Alyn Shipton 2004

Typeset by CA Typesetting, Sheffield
Printed and bound in Great Britain by Antony Rowe, Chippenham, Wiltshire

British Library Cataloguing in Publication Data
A catalogue record for this book is available from the British Library

Library of Congress Cataloging in Publication Data
A catalogue record for this book is available on request from the Library of Congress

ISBN 0-415-97257-4 (hbk)

contents

introduction and acknowledgements

Jazz pianists occupy a unique place in the story of jazz, and the development of the solo piano tradition can be traced independently from that of instrumental ensemble jazz. Above all, piano jazz is about the musicians who have made their own individual contributions to the style, and in this collection I have drawn together a selection of my conversations with some of the key practitioners. Mainly spanning the period from the birth of bebop to the present, but with old masters such as Sir Charles Thompson looking back at the swing era, and repertory specialist Butch Thompson looking even further back, their collective experience is a major part of jazz piano history.

I have been fascinated with the sound of jazz piano since I first scrambled onto my parents' piano stool as a small child, and tried to make for myself some of the sounds I had heard on my father's record collection. I can't pretend that I was ever much of a jazz pianist, but at least I learned enough to know just what skill and effort had gone into the playing of those I admired most. In the end, after studying the classical cello, and then graduating to the double bass, I was privileged to play alongside some of my heroes, and if I have one regret it is that I didn't record or jot down any of the marvellous after-hours conversations I had with the likes of Sing Miller, Alton Purnell, Don Ewell, or any of the others I was lucky enough to work with. I did, fortunately, start recording my conversations with Sammy Price, whom I got to know both from meeting him in New York and working alongside him in Europe, and these were incorporated into his 1989 autobiography *What Do They Want?*

I am most grateful to all the colleagues and organizations who have helped with this book. First and foremost to Jeremy Siepmann and Rhinegold Publishing for permission to reprint articles that have appeared in *Piano* magazine, and equally to Jon Newey, Publishing Director and Stephen Graham, Editor, at Jazzwise Publications for permission to reprint articles that first appeared in *Jazzwise* magazine. I have also reprinted small sections of material from *The Times*, *Jazziz* and London Symphony Orchestra liner notes, which are used with permission.

As will become clear from the preamble to each conversation, many of these meetings came about as a consequence of my work for the BBC, and I am grateful to my producers at Radio 2, Radio 3 and the World Service, Felix Carey, Terry Carter, Derek Drescher, Gabriel Gilson and Oliver Jones, for all the opportunities that have arisen in the course of our work to have lengthy conversations with musicians, once the needs of our various programmes had been met.

Finally a word of thanks to my long-term publisher Janet Joyce at Equinox, and to her colleague Valerie Hall, for their support for the book.

1 carla bley

It is fitting that Carla Bley should, by accident of the alphabet, be the first piece in this collection because she was also my very first interviewee on my weekly BBC World Service *Jazzmatazz* show at the beginning of its six-year run in 1997. The occasion was the release of her big band album *Goes To Church*. The interview that follows dates from the early summer of 2003 and parts of it were published in the July issue of *Piano*, with other sections appearing in the June issue of *Jazzwise*.

With her cascade of silvery blonde hair, her energetic presence conducting her big band, and the studied air she brings to her keyboard playing, Carla Bley is one of the most distinctive and immediately recognizable figures in contemporary jazz. An iconoclastic composer, whose work spans free jazz, rock fusion, and conventional big-band orchestration, she is hard to pigeonhole in the way that jazz critics like to do, so the inescapable conclusion is that she is a one-off, a genuine original. The release in June 2003 of *Looking For America* by Carla Bley's Orchestra, marking the band's first appearance on record for seven years, was a good excuse to talk to Carla about her life and work.

The first, and most disarming, thing about her is that she tends to play down her achievements. She was catapulted to fame in the late 1960s as a result of two major compositions, *A Genuine Tong Funeral*, recorded by Gary Burton in 1967–68, and *Escalator Over The Hill*, a vast quasi-operatic leviathan written with librettist Paul Haines, which took over three years to record with an all-star cast. *Escalator* is now chiefly remembered for the visionary scale of Carla's music, rather than the advanced hippiedom of the lyrics. But although her compositional skill has been compared to that of Duke Ellington, she doesn't see it that way at all.

"I've never pushed at a single boundary on purpose," she says. "I seem to have succeeded in doing so, but actually I find it quite a shock that I have what's called an 'individual style.' I aim at doing something I think is typical, based on the kind of orchestration Ellington was doing before I was born, with four trumpets, four trombones and five reeds, and people

Carla Bley talking to the author at the BBC in 1997 (Derek Drescher)

tell me it isn't ordinary. But it is to me. I suppose I try to stay within the boundaries and fail miserably!"

For her, composition is not an instant business. She chips away at it every day, until pieces take shape, often over a long period of time. "In the mid-1990s," she says, "I was commissioned to write something for the Berlin Festival. I was wondering what to write, and I picked up a fragment of a piano piece by another musician, just a little musical idea. Overall, it took three years to work it into a score for the big band. I called it *Setting Calvin's Waltz*, and that's exactly what the piece is about. It's the truth about composing turned into a musical narrative."

She is also quite willing to admit that many of her pieces don't work. "A lot of what we do as composers is a consequence of our inability to do anything else," she believes. "On the new album there's a series of short pieces linked by the theme of motherhood. In fact, they were sections of an unsuccessful larger composition, which I simply could not make hang together. So, for the album, I decided to let them stay in separate parts, and consequently these several short movements divide up the longer pieces on the disc.

"When I write, I begin at the piano, teasing out all the themes, but then I orchestrate at the desk. Once it's all written out, I dread going back to the piano in case I get drawn in another direction. The way in which I write is a process over which I feel I have little control. I just keep going until it's over, and sometimes that does involve taking a new direction."

Although Carla may dread returning to the piano, she takes almost the opposite approach to the way her music develops once the parts are handed out to her band. Playing the pieces live, and allowing them to marinate during a tour is a well-tried method. *Looking For America* took three years to write, evolved on tour in Europe during the summer of 2002, and was actually recorded on Carla's return to the United States, with an American line-up plus her regular European sidekicks Andy Sheppard and Wolfgang Pushnig, who were flown in to join the sax section.

"Taking a big band on the road nowadays is not an easy proposition," she says. "We usually only travel if we're going to record. More often than not, instead of touring, Steve Swallow and I fly to somewhere in Europe with a collection of scores, and play my music with a bunch of local players. It works well musically, it's a reasonably inexpensive option for promoters, and so the whole thing makes sense. But when it comes to doing an album, I think it makes equal musical and financial sense to travel, and this recording was done in New York after we'd played all the repertoire on the road. Although the eventual session involved some different musicians from those on the tour, I'd really had the chance to hear how all the music sounded in a variety of contexts."

One thing I noticed about the major set-piece on *Looking For America*, her riotous arrangement that intertwines *The Star Spangled Banner*, *O Canada* and a new theme of her own into the *National Anthem* suite, was the frequent emergence of her piano, particularly playing some fragmented arpeggiated figures between the full orchestral sections. It's also prominently featured in her joyous reworking of *Old Macdonald Had A Farm*.

Yet, rather as she likes to downplay her skills as a composer, she does the same as a pianist, despite three duo albums with bassist Steve Swallow, and a trio disc that added Andy Sheppard to their partnership, all of which reveal that she has comparable individuality as an instrumentalist to that which she enjoys as a composer. Yet for someone who spends as much time as she does touring the world's jazz festivals as a headline act, she has a refreshing modesty about her own ability.

"I am just in awe at most of the festivals we play," Carla says. "I listen to the other bands, and I just can't believe the level of playing. I haven't given up trying to be a pianist, and I practise every day, but I can't see my ideas through in the same way as I can as a composer. I might be starting a solo, when I have a great idea and start to develop it. Pow! But once I get to about the tenth bar, I find I want to do something I just don't have the chops to do, so I flutter around a bit and give up. For the most part, I just give myself short solos now. I remember from way back when I was working with Gary Burton, he used to say to his students 'Always finish your solo with a flourish!' I thought to myself, 'A flourish. That's something fast, something smart!' So I began to work on flourishes, but I still find they tend to come at the beginning, rather than the end of my solos."

One strategy she has developed with the big band is to play alongside another pianist or organist, more often than not her daughter, Karen Mantler. "That works very well," she agrees, "because I need more hands than I have available to play what I'm hearing in my brain. I'm fascinated by the combination of organ and piano, and having the pair of us at two keyboards is like 'one big me.' The same is true with most of the keyboard players I've added to the line-up over the years, except for the eight-piece band with Larry Goldings that made my *4 x 4* album in 1999, where his musical personality was so strong that the two of us were 'one big him'!"

But surely, I persist, she must be rather proud of her playing on a duo album such as her 1998 *Are We There Yet?* It not only threw her piano playing into sharp relief, but also seemed to me to have a rather higher flourish quotient than she was suggesting she normally achieved. However, from what she has just said, this can't have been something she particularly enjoyed.

"No, you're right. I'm not ever going to do that again! Making that album was very hard for me. We recorded what must have been about nineteen gigs, just to get those six or seven tunes. Not all the concerts were successful in my terms, and I guess eventually we chose the performances from those places where I'd managed a bit of a flourish at the end! Seriously, I'd rather direct a double orchestra than play duo again."

Her current big band might not be a double orchestra exactly, but it is a nineteen-piece band, and it certainly sounds like an even larger force on the aforementioned *National Anthem* suite, an extended composition that deconstructs twenty-first century patriotic North American songs with the same verve that Charles Ives brought to his orchestral works *Fourth of July* or *Decoration Day* in the early twentieth century. Had Carla intended to play such musical games with her national heritage?

"Actually, no. I just kept going writing this piece until it was over. I have no control over the direction a composition takes once I start to work on it. I didn't set out to include *The Star Spangled Banner*, and in fact I was developing the first theme, which is an original piece of mine, when I realized that the two numbers shared the same opening notes. So I started by just popping in the opening line of *Star Spangled Banner* as a quote, but as the next three months went by and I worked further on the piece, that tune began to creep in further and further to the whole fabric of the composition, so that the entire second section became *The Star Spangled Banner*. There was nothing I could do to stop it, or to hold the irreverent stuff in check, except that I got rather misty-eyed towards the end, and it became quite beautiful.

"I have to say that I wrote this number, and conceived the *Looking For America* album, way before the recent events in US foreign policy that led to the war in Iraq. Last summer [2002], wherever we went, we played *National Anthem*, in Europe, and even in South Korea. One thing I was happy about, given the kinds of noises that were coming out of America even then, was that while we were playing it, nobody threw anything. Sometimes after the concerts people would come up and ask, 'Why?' But since Iraq, I'm not going to be playing it so much.

"I guess I'm going to have to change the whole suite if American foreign policy continues to go in the direction it has been. What a strange artistic dilemma – to have to change your work according to what George W. Bush does! I've already changed it since I first wrote it, when it had a much more sarcastic ending, with an abbreviated return to *The Star Spangled Banner*. In concert last year, that was a musical joke that simply didn't work, and so that's where the soft, sad ending came from. But I suppose now I could make it angry!"

So far because we have focused so much on this one piece, I feel our conversation is in danger of implying that it is almost the only thing on the album, which is, it seems to me, a much more structured entity than some of her other recent discs, harking back to some of her earlier through-composed albums such as *A Genuine Tong Funeral* or *Escalator Over The Hill*. Has she made a conscious effort to conceive the entire album as a whole?

"Yes, it is a more 'written' album, not just a bunch of tunes. That's partly because of the four short 'mother' pieces that are interspersed between the longer ones, which have the function of drawing the rest of the album together."

This leads us into a digression about whether jazz magazines ought to create regular opportunity for musicians to reply to their reviewers, as a matter of course. Carla feels that critics often raise questions in their reviews that ask things such as "What are those four pieces with 'Mother' in the title doing there? Why were only ten musicians used on this section? What is the point of the coda on such-and-such a piece..." These never get answered, except sometimes in the letters column a month or two later, by which time everyone has forgotten the review.

"I'd like to reply to my critics," she says, "and give the real reasons for doing things. So often these get lost in supposition and opinion."

I counter by suggesting that some of her pieces have such a strong narrative element about them that there's no chance of mistaking what they're about. For instance, a piece on this disc called *Tijuana Traffic* uses a lot of elements of Mexican music to describe the mayhem of life on the road in Mexico. It's an atmosphere that's a lot more gritty and realistic than the jolly sounds of Herb Alpert's *Tijuana Taxi* which it occasionally deliberately echoes.

"It's funny you should say that because I recently got a copy of *The Best Of The Tijuana Brass*. Some of those pieces start absolutely brilliantly, with great crispness and precision, and then they just sink into total nothingness. I love a couple of the tunes and the opening sections, but I guess really Herb Alpert had no more idea than I have about real Mexican music – we both latched onto the rhythm and to some of the brilliance and flair of the trumpet style. But my piece gets away from the Alpert sound pretty quickly! After all the middle section is about a car crash, a near-death experience, and Lew Soloff almost doesn't recover.

"Actually the story, the sequence of events, came to me after I'd written the piece, but to get Lew to play the way I wanted, I had to tell him the story. I said, 'Lew, can you please not sound so triumphant at the end? You're almost dead!' Normally Lew can't do anything else but be triumphant. He's such a magnificent trumpeter, that's the way he is. Or if you ask him to play quietly, he takes it as a technical challenge and plays with no energy at all so you can hardly hear him. But this really worked, and the more he got into it the more he sounded deflated, which was what I wanted. You really feel he's been hurt at the end of his solo."

If this story had come to her after she'd written the bulk of the piece, had her earlier strongly narrative pieces followed a similar pattern, with the story coming after the music?

"Almost always, yes. I suppose the best example was *Escalator Over The Hill*, where the story was created a long, long time after the piece was finished."

I wonder if Carla's ability to tell stories in music is helped by the consistent core of soloists with whom she's worked over the years, and who appear on the new album, as they did on *Goes To Church* and on *4 x 4*, namely Soloff, Wolfgang Pushnig, Andy Sheppard and the rambunctious Gary Valente.

"Undoubtedly, and you'd have to add Steve Swallow to that list as well because in any of our groups Steve takes the drummer in hand, and I sit over the organ player. Once the rhythm section is functioning, everything else just falls into place, but of course those four front-line soloists are a key ingredient, too. In fact we're going into the Iridium in New York for a week in June [2003] to play the music from the album, but neither Andy nor Wolfie can make it. It'll be my American band, much as on the disc, but although I was able to fly those two over for the recordings, sadly they can't make the album launch, so it's going to be interesting working with different musicians in those roles."

This brings me to a final observation about the new album, which is how well it harnesses Steve Swallow's talents – not just anchoring the rhythm section, but soaring up into his high register, setting complex lines and creating the kind of warm textures that few other bass guitarists can even get near.

"Well, of course, I know what he can do. He complains a lot when he has to look away from the music and watch his fingerboard to see where I've sent him, when I write stuff for his very highest range, which means, of course, that he has to memorize the music. In fact, although he does a lot of high register stuff here, it's not as high as I was pushing him to play a year or two ago. I've brought him down about a third, but it's worth it because of everything else that enables him to do. When you live and work alongside someone for a long time, you think you know what you're going to get, but he can still surprise us all!"

As our conversation draws to a close, I realize that however much she downplays her playing or her composing, Carla has one thing in common with every other innovator in jazz, which is that she's always looking forwards. Her best album is always the latest, and her greatest excitement is reserved for what's coming next.

2 joanne brackeen

This interview was written for the May/June 2003 issue of *Piano*, when JoAnne Brackeen had just paid a long overdue return visit to Britain, appearing at Ronnie Scott's. I knew her work from records, but had not heard her playing live until that week at the London club. Reviewing her opening night for *The Times*, I wrote:

> There's a process of improvising that the late Earl Hines used to call "concertising." It meant taking a jazz solo and adding all the trimmings of a bravura classical cadenza, testing the extremes of the piano's volume and range, and contrasting playing of great delicacy with ruggedly pounded chords. JoAnne Brackeen's unaccompanied version of *Body And Soul* was a brilliant example of this technique in action. A swirly introduction gradually crystallized into the well-known melody, which was then alternately caressed and pulverized, with some audacious passing harmonies thrown in.

> Despite her gentle, schoolmarm-ish appearance – her hair wound up into a bun, her floppy cardigan and her legs swinging rhythmically under the piano stool – Brackeen is a musical tigress, and her current quartet is every bit as impressive as her solo playing. An infrequent visitor to London, she never fails to surprise with the power and invention of her work, which is based both on the radical re-examination of standards and her own knotty compositions, most of which are catchily eccentric.

Shortly after that notice appeared, the interview below took place.

"Art Blakey played like a man from the jungle, and his band was his tribe," laughs JoAnne Brackeen, looking back on the moment in 1969 when she broke through from playing with local bands around Los Angeles to join the big league. "Our first concert was in Tokyo, and the band came on and played three or four numbers. Then suddenly I hear Art at the microphone announcing that I am going to play a solo, and immediately the rest of the band march off stage. I didn't know anything about it before-

JoAnne Brackeen at London's Pizza Express Jazz Club (Derek Drescher)

hand, and I had no time to think. I just launched into something and played. It was the defining moment in my career. I took so much energy from Art's playing at the drums that it saw me through and that energy remains with me. I think it accounts for the way I am now, and even today I only rehearse enough with my band so that everyone knows what the tune is and one or two of the ways we might tackle it, but the rest is down to the stimulus of the moment."

JoAnne Brackeen is one of the most versatile and wide-ranging pianists in contemporary jazz. Her voracious appetite for new musical experience has taken her into every style of the music from the straightforward to the completely free, but in whatever context she plays with ferocious energy and commitment, willing those around her to raise their game, or, if she is playing solo, drawing her audience directly into the experience of spontaneous creation. She is making a rare visit to Britain to play at Ronnie Scott's, and she has just released a new quartet album recorded at the Jazz Standard in New York, infused with her characteristic intensity.

"Before I played with Art," she recalls, "I had already done occasional gigs with leading players like bassist Paul Chambers or drummer Billy Higgins. But nothing had prepared me for Blakey's energy and power.

He didn't apply this to anything I'd written; in fact I'd say that my pieces were generally too hard for him as they involved different metres and some complex structures, so everything came from the way we tackled our standard repertoire. I had never played with a group or in a situation like it. It was my first contact with real musical energy, and I took to it so much that Art used to call me his 'adopted daughter'! I think that was the moment I became the 'new me,' and when I left Art's band in 1972, I felt it was down to me to supply the energy that I used to draw from him."

It's easy to hear the way she harnesses that power in her solo concerts, but how does it work in a band?

She pauses, and then says, "I can think of a good example just a week or two ago, when I had to play with the student band I direct at the New School in Manhattan. For some reason our usual pianist couldn't make it and he hadn't had time to fix for another student to cover for him, so I sat down at the piano. I'd played maybe a couple of notes when the bassist said, 'Wow! What a sound! It's nothing like what I'm used to hearing.' Back in the days of Blakey's band, that's what every jazz pianist had. In other words, we developed our own unique sound, something that made it immediately obvious who was playing, and mine was all about capturing that energy from Art.

"Today, with my students, I find it difficult to get them to develop their own individual sound, however good they are, but it's something I have myself as a result of coming up through the bebop era. All of us who were active in the sixties and seventies have arrived at our own sound: Chick Corea, Keith Jarrett, Herbie Hancock. I think Herbie was without doubt one of the strongest sounds of our era, with wonderful feeling in his playing, and when he focuses on jazz these days he still has it. Occasionally I've heard him working with a mediocre rhythm section, but within a minute or two you're no longer listening to them, all you hear is him."

At this point I suggest that there is a paradox in Brackeen's career because according to most of the biographies I've read about her, at an early age she turned her back on a formal musical education, preferring to teach herself; yet here she is today, lecturing at the New School in New York or at Berklee in Boston.

"Oh, I never had anything against education. It's just that when I was growing up there really was none. The first schools teaching jazz were only just beginning, and they were nowhere near the West Coast. When I was young, new things occurred to me every day to work on, and I never stopped progressing. I did win a scholarship to the Los Angeles Conservatory of Music, and I loved my piano lessons there. I actually took six months of classical piano tuition, but I dropped all the rest of the classes because they were just repeats of what I had already done."

So how does she think that compares with the experience of the students she teaches today?

"Because there's schooling available for jazz players from the age of eleven or twelve, many of them come into Berklee sounding great already. At the other extreme, I get some students who are fine pianists, but they really don't know anything about jazz. A good example is one current student who comes from Spain. I had him marked down as little more than a fairly good pianist until we were working on Chick Corea's piece *Spain*. Suddenly his playing was fantastic – I'd never heard him playing anything Hispanic, only his efforts at trying to learn bebop. He couldn't easily bring his skills from one genre to another, and that became a challenge for me as his teacher. It's constantly exciting to be teaching at Berklee, where they have so many students from all over the world, and it's no exaggeration to say that I come into contact with one or two geniuses a semester. I teach a piano master class there, working on my students' solo playing as well as working with a rhythm section of bass and drums."

Between classes at the New School in Manhattan and her weekly shuttle to Boston, Brackeen takes off for club sessions and concerts round the United States, and occasional overseas visits, such as her current visit to England. How much of this is solo, and how much in an ensemble?

"Some years, and this is a good example with my London appearance and a residency earlier in the year at the Jazz Standard in New York, it seems like it's all quartet work. But then a period will come along when I seem to be doing nothing but solo concerts, and I find myself longing for a quartet session or to play some trio or duo dates. I actually love playing in duos because it involves a different kind of dynamic between me and the other musician. Just recently I did a week of duos with saxophonist Ravi Coltrane at the Jazz Bakery in Los Angeles, and that was a lot of fun. I think it was very different for both of us, as he'd not done it before, and I tend to work more often with a bass player as the other member of the duo, rather than a saxophonist. I still do duos with bassist Cecil McBee, who was in my earliest trio, and I sometimes also get the chance to play duos with Eddie Gomez on bass, who was in a later version of my group. Both of those bassists are wonderful creative partners, and so, too, is Ray Drummond, but I think he's less comfortable with some of the unusual metres I like to use, like five and seven."

This brought up the subject of JoAnne's most recent solo album, *Popsicle Illusion*, made in 1999, which opens with a 7/4 version of Frank

Loesser's song *If I Were A Bell*. The change of metre itself is not so remarkable because plenty of modern jazz musicians like to move well-known tunes out of their even four-to-the-bar feel into something more challenging, but Brackeen's treatment is noticeably different because she has chosen to do this within the Harlem stride style of the 1920s. It's a dazzling feat, and for much of the opening chorus, she keeps what sounds like a four-four stride pattern going in her left hand, until you realize she is displacing the tune above it in 7/4 time, so the downbeat seldom falls where the left-hand pattern suggests it does. Then, just as you adjust your ear to that, she slips in one of the left-hand turnarounds that the Harlem masters used to adopt, by repeating a pedal note, rather than keeping a simple oom-pah rhythm going. Consequently the expected return to the pattern jumps by a beat, as she plays "oom-pah-oom-pah-oom-oom-pah." This is tricky stuff, and I want to know how she arrived at the idea.

"I don't really know. I just thought it would be fun to stride in seven. I don't know if anyone's done it before, but it seems to me to have plenty of opportunities. I don't really keep the stride left hand going beyond the first couple of choruses. I move on into regular 7/4 playing after that, but of course it could be developed in its own right. If someone could keep it up and build on it throughout an entire number that would be fantastic!"

The title track of that solo disc, *Popsicle Illusion*, turns up again as a quartet number on her latest quartet album. Isn't it rather strange to repeat a tune from one album to the next, even though, admittedly, the instrumental and solo versions are very different?

"I think once it's written, a composition exists separately from any of us, so it can be played in any format. When I play solo, I hear the piano as if it were an orchestra, so I hear the tune the same way, whatever format I'm actually working in."

Certainly the tune is difficult enough to warrant the inclusion of the quartet version on her new disc, with Ravi Coltrane, bassist Ira Coleman and drummer Horacio "El Negro" Hernandez working their way impressively through its myriad twists and turns, each as unexpected as the slippery texture and shape of the confectionery it is named after. Certainly Brackeen is very proud of her current quartet, but then so she should be, having worked in two of the greatest jazz quartets of the last quarter century, with tenorists Joe Henderson and Stan Getz.

"I worked with Joe for much, much longer than it says in all my biographies," she says. "I was with him from 1972 to 1986, although for the last part of that time I was also leading my own band, so Joe hired other pianists. I'd love to have played with him again, when he had his final period of international fame in the 1990s, but that never happened. Stan, on the other hand, made me hypercritical of saxophonists. After working with him I can't bear anyone to be the slightest bit out of tune. I always treated him as if I was playing for a vocalist. I had all the power he needed when he opened up to play jazz, but for his ballads he needed the same delicacy and sensitivity as the very best singer. It was wonderful to play for someone whose music was so perfect."

3 dave brubeck

In common with most of the generation that grew up in the 1950s and 1960s, for me the Brubeck Quartet became part of the aural backdrop to life. My schoolfriends and I exchanged copies of *Unsquare Dance*, *Take Five* or *Blue Rondo À La Turk* along with discs from the nascent British pop scene, and their sounds became lodged in my subconscious. I first met Dave Brubeck himself in the spring of 1994, when I was covering the piano festival at the Regattabar in Cambridge, Massachusetts, for *The Guardian* and BBC Radio 3, and Dave had just returned to playing fairly small venues, following his recovery from a mysterious viral illness during 1993. Since then we've worked on several broadcasts together, and I was privileged to be asked by Dave to write notes for his fortieth anniversary UK tour album and his eightieth birthday collaboration with the London Symphony Orchestra. This piece conflates two conversations, the first of which is drawn from those eightieth birthday celebrations in 2000. The second took place on the lawns at Tanglewood a couple of years later, shortly before a storming set from Dave's quartet, which held the vast crowds entranced, despite the onset of an autumnal drizzle. It was published in the January 2003 edition of *Piano*.

December 2000 was a landmark month in the long career of pianist Dave Brubeck, as he celebrated his eightieth birthday with two very unusual concerts at the Barbican Hall in London, accompanied by the London Symphony Orchestra (LSO) and a rather special jazz septet. With all four of his sons, Darius, Chris, Matthew and Dan in the line-up, plus two members of his regular touring band, British bassist Alec Dankworth and saxophonist Bobby Militello, there was a close sense of family feeling about the group. And that sense of family extended both to Dave's long-term associate, manager, producer and conductor Russell Gloyd, and to the LSO as well, following the immense success of his concerts with the orchestra in 1990 and 1995. The Barbican Hall itself also played a part in

Dave Brubeck and the author, Bath Festival, 1997 (Derek Drescher)

the flavour of this family occasion, as it had previously been the setting for Dave's seventieth and seventy-fifth birthday celebrations.

The whole idea of family has been fundamental to Brubeck's musical life from the outset, from the days of his childhood on a vast cattle ranch in California, where his mother brought him up, along with his brothers Henry and Howard, to believe that any music heard around the house was best if it was made by the boys themselves. Although his own sons were raised in a less isolated environment, where all kinds of music were brought into their home and listened to intently, they, too, started their musical training young, although Dave and his wife Iola had no intention of grooming any of them to become jazz musicians from an early age. However, one way or another, and some sooner than others, his boys found their own routes into the jazz world and the jazz life, which may not be all that surprising following an upbringing where, owing to their father's career, they rubbed shoulders not just with any old jazz players, but the world's very finest exponents of the genre, from Louis Armstrong and Miles Davis to Count Basie and Duke Ellington.

As his sons grew in musicianship and maturity, Dave worked with various permutations of younger Brubecks over the years, but it was not until December 1993 that all four brothers recorded with their father, when they were all marooned at the family home in Connecticut, where Dave had planned to record his regular group in a nearby hall. "Telarc were all set up to make the disc, and my producer John Snyder and the crew were all staying nearby," Dave told me. "It was already showing signs of being a very severe winter, when a couple of days after Christmas there was a sudden snow and ice storm, and there was no way the other members of my usual quartet could travel the forty miles or so from New York. But there were two pianos sitting in the hall, and my sons were all home for Christmas. They're never in the same place together very often, so I thought we'd take a chance."

The resulting album, *In Your Own Sweet Way*, was the beginning of a collaboration that has flourished again in the succeeding years, despite the family's geographical separation, with Dave in Connecticut or frequently on tour, Darius in South Africa, Matthew in California, and the other two brothers travelling widely, both in their own individual projects and with the "Brubeck Brothers" band that they formed in 1996.

The family's occasional get-togethers during the second half of the 1990s coincided with one of the most fertile periods of Dave's whole career, both as pianist and composer, where he cast aside any sense of advancing years by creating a collection of new music that is as tough, original and aggressively modern as anything he has ever produced. Nevertheless, as those of us who were privileged to attend his fortieth anniversary tour of the UK in 1998 will have witnessed, even the most startling of his new numbers such as *Salmon Strikes* was played alongside a smattering of far more familiar fare.

To my mind, quite apart from the strong filial ties apparent at his birthday concert, another reason for the strong sense of family connections in Dave Brubeck's own work over the years is that his core repertoire itself has consolidated into a familiar group of compositions that he has regularly reinvestigated and rediscovered. A good example is his famous composition from the 1950s, *In Your Own Sweet Way*, which was not only the title track of the disc by Dave and his four sons, but a piece he recorded in the 1990s as a piano duet with George Shearing, and which also found its way into his LSO eightieth birthday concert programme as a feature both for Dave's own piano and the cello playing of his youngest son Matthew.

That's not to say that his repertoire is in any way narrow or limited. Indeed, Dave himself was surprised at its extent when bassist Alec Dankworth joined his quartet in 1998 and had to start learning the repertoire. "I met a record collector on one of our first English concerts with Alec, who says he has 150 of my albums," he recalled. "I only knew of about 130 of them myself, so he obviously had lots of foreign issues and bootlegs, but the point is that if each of them has ten different tunes on average, then, to get to know the book, Alec has to be familiar with 1,500 numbers!"

Nevertheless, among that total there are some pieces that are played more often than others, and the idea of constantly reworking his compositions has been a feature of Dave's work since the days of his very first experimental octet from 1949, a band that not only came under the direct influence of Dave's composition teacher Darius Milhaud, but which included two of his most famous collaborators, clarinettist Bill Smith, who has often been a member of Dave's touring quartet in the half-century since, and altoist Paul Desmond, who became a key member of the most famous Brubeck quartet of all, during much of the 1950s and 1960s.

It is hard to realize today just how revolutionary this quartet was, back in those years. Nowadays, most competent jazz musicians can breeze through a whole range of time signatures without a second thought, but in the late 1950s, when Dave began introducing unusual metres to jazz for more or less the first time, from 5/4 and 9/8 to 11/4, this ran so contrary to the normal notions of 4/4 swing that even the most experienced jazz players found thinking and counting in uneven numbers of beats to be a challenge.

It was a challenge that the Brubeck quartet itself dismissed with nonchalant ease. On its 1959 album *Time Out*, the group showed its mastery of playing, improvising and above all, swinging, in a whole range of metres. Most famous of all was Paul Desmond's piece *Take Five*, which is reputed to have become the first million-selling jazz instrumental, and which it seems Dave must have played almost as many times as it has sold copies over the years. It made an appearance on the eightieth birthday Barbican concert, as did another piece from the same original album, Dave's own *Blue Rondo À La Turk* (written in 9/8 with a pulse of 2 + 2 + 2 + 3), in which the rhythm section's jazz playing was set amid some brisk and aggressive orchestral scoring. Another piece from *Time Out* that featured that night was the immortal *Three To Get Ready*, during which the *Daily Telegraph* critic noted the Barbican audience happily nodding and foot tapping along with a time-signature of 7/4!

From the days of his studies with Milhaud in the 1940s, Dave has always been interested in the territory where improvising jazz musicians encounter the tonal depth and texture of the symphony orchestra. In 1959, the same year as *Time Out*, he also recorded his *Dialogues For Jazz Combo and Orchestra*, which was one of his first full-scale ventures in this direction. Dave proved immediately that he had a tremendous talent for orchestral writing. His eightieth birthday concert displayed this talent at its height, with a magnificent handling of instrumental timbres ranging from the pizzicato strings and oboe that contrasted with the jazz drumset, alto sax and piano of *Summer Music*, to the elegant classicism of the orchestral opening to *Chorale* that framed some of Dave's most reflective and modernistic piano playing.

At the centre of those birthday evenings was the octogenarian himself, who became the subject of the highlight of the entire event, the world premiere of Darius Brubeck's *Four Score In Seven* – a piece inscribed by its composer as "for sons to play on Dave's eightieth birthday." From its opening abstraction to the rock inflections of its later sections, this was a cannily crafted reflection of many of the musical aspects that have made Dave Brubeck's first eighty years so special for so many of us. But most special of all is the sense that although this was a public concert, this premiere had made us all part of a very intimate and closely-knit family event.

Almost two years on from that concert, I caught up with Dave again at the Tanglewood Jazz Festival, a joyous weekend that takes place at the end of the annual Boston Symphony Orchestra summer season at the orchestra's outdoor home in the Berkshire Hills.

This festival is the brainchild of Massachusetts entrepreneur Fred Taylor, who runs the celebrated Sculler's club in Boston, but whose friendship with Dave goes back half a century to the days of George Wein's old club in the city, called Storyville.

"He snuck in what must have been the first portable tape recorder I ever saw, hid it under the table, and recorded us on the sly," recalled Dave, chuckling at the memory. "It would not have gone down too well with George Wein, if he had known about it at the time! That particular day, my drummer and bassist were both sick, and so it ended up being the first occasion that saxophonist Paul Desmond and I played an entire set of duets. Fred got all of it on tape, and in due course he did a deal with Columbia records and it was issued. To this day, I think it's beautiful, with Paul playing really great stuff, and the two of us just improvising like crazy to compensate for the lack of the other two guys.

"And my association with Tanglewood goes back almost as far as my friendship with Fred because at the old Music Barn at Lenox, which is on the edge of the Tanglewood site, we used to get together every summer in the 1950s with people like the Modern Jazz Quartet, Jimmy Giuffre, Gunther Schuller, and Ornette Coleman. We all lived and played in the barn, and Bill Smith, my clarinet player in my very first group, was a teacher at the Lenox Summer School that the MJQ pianist John Lewis organized there. So we had a reason to spend part of our summers here, and I've been coming ever since!"

The huge crowd that braved a rather damp night to sit on the acres of lawn that surround the new Ozawa Hall at Tanglewood, and listen to Dave's current quartet as the sun set over the distant hills, was evidence of Brubeck's continued popularity after such a long association with the venue. But his popularity is not confined to rural America because his present band is still pulling in record audiences all over the world. At the same time, Dave is busily engaged in composing and recording his classical works as well. When we met, he'd just received the first tapes of a forthcoming album of his *a capella* pieces for choir, recorded by the Chattanooga Choral Society. He'd also not long finished making an entirely new version of his massive work, *The Gates Of Justice*.

"It's with the Baltimore Symphony and Choral Society, conducted by my old friend and colleague Russell Gloyd, and the quartet plays in it as well," said Dave. "I think the whole thing lasts about fifty minutes. Actually, after I originally recorded it thirty-five years ago, I thought it would never be heard again, once the original disc went out of print because I couldn't get the rights back. But finally after a long battle, I got them, and now I've made this brand new version, which I'm really excited about. On the other hand, I'm just as excited about my ongoing work with the London Symphony Orchestra. During the summer of 2002, I made some studio recordings with them, and at first it was really daunting going into Abbey Road with the Orchestra, the Covent Garden Chorus, my quartet, and a children's choir. I was thinking about all the great composers and conductors who had worked in that same studio, men like Elgar whose picture is on the studio wall. With so much on the line, I was feeling tense about how to get all these elements working together, but they did, and soon we got a real sense of the fun that comes with making music together."

I suggested to Dave that it's this ongoing sense of fun that draws audiences to his quartet appearances throughout the world.

"You just hope it happens," he grinned. "During all the many years I've been playing, I always go out on stage hoping it'll happen again. When it starts, I get really happy. The members of the group I have now like playing together, and that's half the battle. There's Bobby Militello on alto sax and flute, who knew all of Paul Desmond's music when he joined the group, but who is very much his own man as well, never ever copying anything of Paul's but just occasionally hinting at the sound we used to get together. Then there's Randy Jones on drums, originally from Britain, who's been with me for years. And the latest recruit is bassist Michael Moore, who joined recently after another Englishman, Alec Dankworth, the son of John Dankworth and Cleo Laine, left the band after some years with us. You can get great musicians who are no fun to play with because they are egomaniacs. But you can have great guys who are also great people, and I've been fortunate enough to have that. They are so co-operative that they want to play with and for each other and have fun. But they can really play like tigers!"

4 uri caine

One of the most versatile pianists in contemporary jazz is Uri Caine. Born in 1956, his versatility is coupled with an extraordinarily prolific output of recordings and large-scale projects, ranging from out-and-out jazz to his detailed explorations of Bach and Mahler that dig deep into the interstices of the genres, adding a host of additional ideas from Jewish cantors to urban DJs. We met in the mid-1990s when Uri was on tour with the Dave Douglas sextet, and appeared in a broadcast I presented from the Vortex in London, an evening memorable both for the degree to which the piano slipped out of tune during the concert and for the disruption of the band's travel plans by an IRA bomb alert, which left them little or no time for a proper sound-check or rehearsal. After such a memorable meeting, we have kept in touch sporadically, and these two conversations date from the January 2002 edition of *Piano*, and a visit to Uri's New York apartment in March 2003, for a BBC *Radio 2 Arts Programme* interview, shortly before his sojourn as artist in residence at the Cheltenham Jazz Festival in the UK. This was the festival's first attempt at such a residency and it was a resounding success, as I wrote in *The Times* of May 6, 2003:

> The Festival's first artist-in-residence, the American pianist Uri Caine, mingled electronics with his piano trio Bedrock. Four sessions displayed different aspects of Caine's multifarious projects, but this group offered him more opportunity to stretch out and extend his ideas than the tighter structures of his ensembles that explored Mahler and Bach. All of his bands used DJs, and Samon Kawamura with Bedrock was the most musically adept at integrating his turntables with the group. The star turn was the versatile, flamboyant drummer Zach Danziger, simultaneously controlling his sticks and the touchpad of his laptop as he switched from one groove to another.
>
> He and bassist Tim Lefebvre formed the rhythm team for Caine's other groups, reacting brilliantly to the constant changes of mood in the *Goldberg Variations*. Caine uses Bach's harmonic structure to extend the original pieces, some remaining close

to their baroque origins, others abstracted into free jazz, or becoming riotous tangos. Most inspired were the gospel vocals of Barbara Walker, linking the contemporary black church with eighteenth-century chorales.

It was a similar concert appearance that prompted my first published conversation with Uri.

In February 2002, Uri Caine will be bringing a most unusual jazz ensemble to Britain for a single London concert in Magnus Lindberg's series. It is Caine's *Primal Light* project, which reinterprets the music of Gustav Mahler in an improvising jazz context. In 2000, he made a brief tour of the UK for the Contemporary Music Network, playing some of this music, but, he told me, this forthcoming concert will include a lot of new material that has seldom – if ever – been played in public.

"Since I made the first *Primal Light* disc, as the score for a silent movie about Mahler by Franz Winter in 1996, I have recorded a whole additional album that explores *Das Lied Von Der Erde* as a basis for improvisation, and in which I've added Chinese instrumentation along with a jazz ensemble, singers, a cantor and a turntable artist," he said. "That disc has yet to come out, but I'll be playing a lot of the music from it when I come to Britain, and the band for the project will include one of my frequent colleagues in New York, trumpeter Ralph Alessi, and also DJ Olive, who was on the original disc."

Such experimental music might seem a strikingly different departure for a pianist who was most recently in the UK with a conventional piano-bass-drums trio, playing relatively straightforward jazz. Together with bassist Drew Gress and drummer Ben Perowsky, he opened for Charlie Haden during last summer's Barbican Jazz series, and subsequently returned for a short autumn tour. In this context, Caine reveals himself as a hard-swinging pianist, with a keen awareness of the jazz tradition, coupled with some highly original compositions of his own. This group, he tells me, has also recorded a CD, but it has yet to appear. One reason for this is that after a year or so since his last album, *Goldberg*, which took a most un-Jacques Loussier look at J. S. Bach, three other new discs by Caine have suddenly appeared simultaneously from the Winter and Winter label, and they each reveal a different aspect of this remarkably multi-faceted musician.

Ever since his early work back in his home town of Philadelphia in the 1980s, Caine has mastered an extraordinary stylistic range, and he has worked with bebop players such as Donald Byrd and Bobby Watson on the one hand, and experimentalists such as drummer Rashied Ali and clarinettist Don Byron on the other. But his first new disc covers an area that is, in recording terms at least, relatively new for him: solo piano. Called *Solitaire*, the disc was cut at Schloss Elmau, a German castle near Munich, where Caine's fellow pianist Brad Mehldau had recently been greatly impressed with its blend of atmosphere and acoustics.

"It's in the country, not too far from the mountains, and the building's used as a combination of a hotel and a retreat," said Caine, "so it has a very different feel from the sterility of the studio. I sat down and played for two or three days, and recorded everything, and the album's a distillation of that. There are thirteen original tracks, plus one standard and a

Uri Caine at the Barbican, London, 2001 (Derek Drescher)

Beatles tune, but it contrasts with my other work not so much because of the material, but how it is approached. In most of my career, my own playing has been subsumed into the needs of a group, but this focuses on the piano. It's not about layers and textures of sound, which I guess a lot of my work has explored. It strips all that away. I'd never really considered myself a solo pianist, even in my early days in Philadelphia where I played in jazz bars, so this was a real challenge for me."

His next disc, called *Bedrock 3*, looks similar at first glance to his other piano trio projects, but Uri was swift to point out where it was different: "This has Zach Danziger on drums and Tim Lefebvre, bass, and it's a group that plays a lot round New York City. In the downtown scene there, at places like the Knitting Factory, where we play often, people are not so into jazz soloing in the conventional sense. So this is a much denser sound. I play electric piano, there are funk rhythms on the electric bass and drums, and once we'd got the basic material down, we added more stuff in the studio – some extra parts, some different sounds. It's very much a reflection of the current New York scene, and even though there's a piece on there called *Lobby Days*, based on the idea that Zach's father was the lobby pianist for years at the Carlyle Hotel, we've transformed the theme into something that works within our overall approach."

I suppose I shouldn't have been surprised, with someone so wide-ranging and who has such endless curiosity about music, that Uri's third new CD of the current season should delve into an entirely different tradition, but I was genuinely nonplussed by the depth to which *Rio* digs into the music of Brazil. But Uri laughed his deep resonant laugh and said, "Why not? A few years ago I made a disc called *Sidewalks of New York*, and that took in all kinds of aspects of local music and added some of the street sounds. This was an attempt to do the same thing in Rio, after I went there on tour in June last year, and resolved to record with local musicians, in the same spirit as my New York project. It's based round a quintet of piano, drums, percussion, guitar and bass, but we added musicians from a samba group, a local rap group, and some people I met who declaim poetry in public places, with a political edge to their words. So there's all that, and a real cross-section of local styles – I guess you could say that if there's one thing this proves, it's that I like a bit of variety in my CDs!"

> Caine's 2003 Cheltenham residency offered him the opportunity to display similar variety in a series of four concerts and a workshop, each with a different group or musical focus. And so our conversation picked up where we had left off before, on the theme of variety.

"I was very grateful to be given the opportunity to do this," said Uri. "In the year and a bit since we last spoke, the range of music's continued to be varied. Some of it has involved taking more ideas from classical music and interpreting them through improvisation, whereas other aspects of it have involved exploring different areas of jazz itself. At Cheltenham I'll be doing two concerts in the latter vein, one a solo piano concert, something I've begun to do more of since *Solitaire*, and the other will be with the trio Bedrock plus a DJ, to explore drum 'n' bass rhythms and jazz. And then I'll be taking forward my classical explorations, with another pair of concerts. One takes another look at Mahler, and the other distils ideas from my double CD based on Bach's *Goldberg Variations*."

At the Magnus Lindberg concert of the *Primal Light* material, I'd sensed that some of London's South Bank audience were not quite prepared for the radical treatment that Uri had given such well-known works as *Das Knaben Wunderhorn*, the *Kindertotenlieder* and *Das Lied Von Der Erde*, as well as the movement of the "Resurrection" Symphony that had given his project its title. How did Uri think the audiences in a rather upmarket Gloucestershire town were going to respond?

"I don't intend to be disrespectful to Mahler in any way, but what I'm trying to do is use the structures, forms and themes of his music as something that we can improvise with, over or against. Sometimes we're referring to the musical material Mahler was familiar with and listening to. At other times we're not making that connection, but trying to treat his work as a kind of musical abstraction that is then commented on – at least that's the intention. Whether or not it will work all the time, I'm not sure. That's part of the challenge because the music changes. There's a cliché in jazz of taking well-known standards and moving them as far away as possible from their original form, say in the Broadway shows for which they were written maybe fifty years ago. So I view this as the same process, taking structure from Mahler and then having the freedom of improvisation to interact with it."

Ironically, I'd felt that the most dramatic sections of the London performance of the Mahler material I'd heard were not the most overtly improvised, but those quite fully scored sections which, as Uri said, had gone back to the musical world of Mahler himself, of the familiar sounds in which he had grown up. In particular this applied to the movements that introduce a Cantor, whose traditional Jewish singing eerily floats up out of the ensemble: a role taken on disc by Aaron Bensoussan.

"Yes, for our British concerts we work with a Cantor from London called Mosche Haschel who joins us for the Cheltenham Festival," said Uri. "You can't always rely on having the same personnel as on the record, when it comes to live performances of these different projects. But I think it pays to be flexible and adaptable, and I'm lucky because there's a pool of musicians I can draw on who are aware of the breadth of music that these projects encompass. Ralph Alessi, the trumpeter whom we've talked of before, has played with me on and off for a long time, and there's different DJs I've worked with, three of whom are coming to Cheltenham. I enjoy the open possibilities for the music that working with different players offers, in terms of improvisation."

I suggested that the broad sweep of Mahler's music lends itself to widely varying improvisational treatments, but that this is a less obvious course with Bach's *Goldberg Variations*, as they are much more intimate, introspective compositions.

"I think my approach to Bach was originally based on the idea that a theme and variations have a direct corollary with the types of music we do as jazz musicians. I started out by trying to explore the idea that the harmony that underpins the theme is the recurring structure that all the variations are built on, just as we improvise over standards, but Bach's original music is more complex and subtle than that. It brings in all the types of music that he was interested in: dance forms, contrapuntal forms, even styles that we don't normally associate with Bach, although all thirty of these very diverse pieces do use that same harmony. So in a way I tried to do the same, play Bach, improvise with and against it, but adding different forms, modern dance styles, yet all the time keeping sight of that same harmonic framework he was using. I wanted to get a kaleidoscopic view of several different types of music."

One of the better musical jokes of Uri's treatment of the *Goldberg Variations* is the snoring effect produced by DJ Olive: an oblique reference to the variations having originally been commissioned for an insomniac. This prompted me to ask why Uri gives such prominence to the increasing use of DJs in his projects.

"Well," Uri pondered, taking a moment to pause for thought, "first of all when I originally moved to New York from Philadelphia, I had the opportunity to play in a lot of situations where DJs were a part of what was going on. The type of dislocation in the sound world that DJs bring is really fascinating, especially in the Mahler or Bach projects, but it's even the case with the more groove-oriented sound of Bedrock, with Samon Kawamura bringing in samples of different things. So in that sense it is just another part of music-making in the world of improvisation in today's New York scene."

To my mind, one of the disadvantages of Caine's larger-scale projects is that they submerge his very individual voice as a solo pianist, and so this aspect of his work is served better by Bedrock or his solo work. Did he agree?

"I used to play a lot of solo when I started out, just playing in bars, but these days I'm more frequently involved in bigger groups or playing as a sideman. However, as a soloist in the wake of *Solitaire* I'm getting into a lot of stuff I've hardly investigated before, such as some of the pre-bebop jazz styles. I love that era of piano playing, but I've been equally influenced by the avant garde, by players like Cecil Taylor, and I guess my current work tries to combine a lot of those things."

But then we were drawn back into a discussion on how Uri's love of all things diverse places his piano-playing into a lot of different contexts. He learned from Winter and Winter's engineer Adrian von Ripka about creating soundscapes, aural portraits of the kind he attempted in *Rio*, and tried something similar in the open air in Venice. "It was a live recording, and he used the kind of portable set-up where you could move around and tape many things, in the street and so on, and it gave me another idea, as to how to get out of the sterile recording-studio environment." Uri's eyes shone brightly with enthusiasm, and he went on to answer my original question. "This is fantastic in cities where music is part of the city's everyday life. I want to try to bring that feeling into my recordings, and I guess this is what's appealing about being an artist in residence in a festival where movement from place to place and being out and about is part of what goes on. Some audiences may have certain preferences, but other listeners bring different perceptions, perhaps without such rigid demarcations between genres as has been in the case in the past. If mixing these different audiences works as a result of presenting a really wide range of musical options to them, then I hope everyone'll be open to accept it all."

5 alice coltrane

In February 2002, Impulse released a four-CD set entitled *Legacy*, which was an anthology of John Coltrane's recordings drawn from all his various labels, Atlantic, Blue Note, Columbia, Impulse, and Prestige. The same month, Warner Jazz reissued several major albums by his widow, the pianist, harpist and organist Alice Coltrane. She only rarely gives interviews, and I was privileged to talk to her for that month's *Jazzwise*, not least because this was also a time when she was making some of her equally rare public appearances as a musician. As she told me, she only performs occasionally nowadays, preferring to focus her energies on the Foundation dedicated to her late husband.

"2001 was a very special year for the Foundation," she said. "In October we honoured John in his seventy-fifth anniversary year, and we put on a major event at the Beverly Hilton Hotel. It was wonderful: well-attended, full of a cross-section of people from youngsters to professionals, and it pointed the way we want the Foundation to go in the future. For the past fourteen years, we've had a John Coltrane Festival, with several events, maybe a competition. But this fifteenth year we wanted to do something a bit different. In the future we don't just want a competition winner up on stage with some well-known current artists; we want to go further, with scholarships, the opportunity for new talents to record, and recommendations to musicians that can help young players' careers.

"I think the anniversary prompted us to move to a greater scale, where we can help young musicians to promote their musical interest, and work closely with those in education. I've been talking to the University of Southern California, also to UCLA, and trying to find ways that our scholarships will work through these and similar schools, especially those where their teachers are great musicians."

I wondered whether she meant those teachers, such as bassist Reggie Workman at New York's New School, who make positive efforts to introduce Trane's music to young players.

"I mean Reggie, of course, and Yusef Lateef, Kenny Burrell, Charlie Haden, all of whose enthusiasm is a nice confirmation of the music. They like to keep the John Coltrane repertoire going because youngsters everywhere like to play it. Reggie's Coltrane Ensemble in New York is interesting. It's not what you might call a legal entity, trading on the Coltrane name, but it's a great informal setting for players getting to know the music. And there are so many levels to John's music, it's far better to get this hands-on approach with players who really know the music than struggle away on your own trying to come to terms with it."

Had the experience of watching her own son, Ravi, go through the stages from beginner to experienced professional influenced her aims for the Foundation?

"Yes, of course. I guess I'm focusing on the fifteen years or so of his life from when he was in high school to when he began to be recognized as a major player in his own right. None of us who got started in music knew much as teenagers. With Ravi, he started playing clarinet in the high-school band, then he went to Cal Arts (the California Institute for the Arts) and he expanded into playing tenor and soprano. When we give our Foundation competition prize, we want to promote young people like him to have access to seasoned professionals, people who've gone through the music world, and we also want to help the institutions create venues for the young musicians to play. In his case, I knew Ravi would be fine. Elvin got him in his band practically when he came out of school, and when Ravi went off to play with him he learned a lot. He wanted to go. Elvin looked after him, after all he'd known him for years, and it was a good experience."

I noticed that Alice said "none of us," which suggested to me she also had her own experience as a teenage musician in mind when she was setting the agenda for the Foundation's help to young players.

"Yes, that's true. When I look back, it was a long time ago! I got to New York from Detroit well before I was twenty-one, and quite a while before I got my first well-known job playing with Terry Gibbs. My original thought was to go to Juilliard or to the Manhattan School of Music, but my brother Ernest Farrow was a bass player, and he was already there in New York, and through him I got the chance to do some jazz jobs, and it just went from there. It was because of Ernest I got my first gig with Johnny Griffin, who was already a fine, fine tenor player. Griffin's piano player was Barry Harris who was a good friend of my brother, and he offered to turn his job over to me. I told him I'd take it, and before long, by the time I was in my early twenties, I'd played with a lot of major musicians. It was my brother who told me about the job with Terry Gibbs. He'd begun playing in Terry's small group, and later there were other Detroit musicians who came into

Alice Coltrane on a visit to London, 1987 (Peter Symes)

the line-up, for example bassists Herman Wright and Paul Chambers both replaced my brother at different times.

"You see, Terry was strictly from the bebop era. He knew that in Detroit we were all highly bebop orientated. There was nothing modal or freeform in my background. We came out of Charlie Parker and Dizzy Gillespie, and the musicians we'd formed our styles around were the key local players, Milt and the Jackson brothers, plus Elvin Jones and his family. And I think even today it'd be hard to improve on that bop background. Learning to play that music gives you a strong focus. I learned all the standards, the ballads, everything from the semi-classics to Broadway shows, and it was, if I look back on it, a pretty strategic kind of study. It's paying your dues. All that work goes into forming your own style."

Hearing Alice say this, it struck me as something of a paradox that her own reputation, apart from her three or four albums with Gibbs, is built on music that seems fundamentally different from the Detroit bebop on which she started out. But, of course, I'd reckoned without the huge influence of John Coltrane himself.

"I met John when Terry Gibbs was playing at Birdland in New York. When I began working with John, and started playing freeform, it gave me another plateau entirely on which to work. He knew everything about the Parker era – after all he'd worked with Dizzy. But he saw higher vistas, higher echelons to reach. Look at what happened to McCoy Tyner's playing while he was with John. His playing was so beautiful, such an enhanced musical experience, that to me it seems as if John made McCoy become an innovator, to develop his playing to a standard where it was followed by many other pianists. But all that came from John. He had a concept of how you would sound, but he never told you how to play or stated what would take place – you developed your own way through his music, and you heard innovation happening. Take Jimmy Garrison, too. He made a huge leap in his playing once I came into the band. He had to be open-minded, to move his own playing onto a higher level."

We talked a bit more about how Garrison had moved from playing supremely accurate walking basslines, almost always playing "time," to someone who could accommodate a much looser concept of metre. I suggested to Alice that although she had moved into the piano chair alongside Garrison, and they worked together with Elvin and then Rashied Ali on a new approach to time, nevertheless following McCoy must have been daunting.

"Not really because John was showing us something on a higher level that took many, many years to reach, and I appreciated it so much. You see, I don't think I ever left anything behind from my earlier way of playing. After all, it gave me a foundation to build on, but soon I was making music a different way. I remember one day John saying to me that it sounded as if I'd been playing this way all my life. I felt that was a great compliment, coming from him."

I knew from speaking to Rashied Ali that, when he first joined the band, Coltrane kept Elvin Jones alongside him in the line-up. Indeed, the original plan had been for the two drummers to continue to play together. What did Alice think about this, having worked with them both?

"I think Rashied did exceptionally well. He developed a rhythmical kind of vibrational approach to the music, which was like a component of what John was hearing. But the other form of approach was a component also. Elvin completed what was needed with a totally different approach. To me he lifted the music; he gave soloists something they have to progress through. It made them come out fiery because he played what was almost like a flourish of notes or beats, and the soloist had to go on through it. Rashied, on the other hand, was very sensitive, very responsive, and he creates a kind of freedom by not defining the steps a soloist must take, where you don't always need to know where 'one' is, but where he gives you a route to the upper causeway, and I thought that was so beautiful.

"In my later career, this approach became very much a part of me. I believed strongly in what John had been doing, and it was as much a part of me as it had been of him. I still feel that, and in my playing there's no returning to the past, other than the occasional reminiscence.

"One way that John had a profound influence on me was that he purchased a harp for me to play. But it was being built the traditional way, by hand, and by the time it was completed, he had left this world. For that reason, when I began to play the harp, it was something particularly close to me – but I don't play it as much now, any more."

So what kind of playing does Alice undertake now?

"I love electronics and synthesizers – things that enhance your sound. But of course the Steinway concert grand sounds so great I never tire of that. Nowadays I do absolutely no playing professionally any more. But I do appear from time to time, like at the Foundation events, or at a retrospective, like when Terry Gibbs invited me to join him on a reminiscence event, and I agreed. That was a beautiful evening, around the time of the Foundation concert, which was also beautiful, with my boys up there on stage as well."

As we talked about this gathering of so many people, owing to a shared interest in John Coltrane, I wondered how she felt about the new four-CD *Legacy* set that Ravi has put together for Universal, licensing in material from all areas of Coltrane's career, and also including several previously unissued tracks.

"The beautiful part is that much of that music is now over forty years old, but that it was and still is such incredible music. The performances were magnificent, and everyone achieved so much and was so creative. There's a timelessness about it. You never hear it and think 'Oh, that's a nice old piece.' Those thoughts never come into your head, and instead it dazzles you with its newness and freshness. Even on the songs that he repeated over and over like *My Favorite Things*, every performance is superb and different. Many youngsters have never heard music like this. John was doing things that would take years to come. I often wonder if he had perfected the things he was working on at home, whether he might have created another new era of music, a next phase that we haven't heard yet. When he was practising in the house, you'd hear all kinds of things going on. It wasn't easy for him to be content. You'd hear something absolutely wonderful one evening, but it was gone by the next day. And if you asked him about it, he'd shrug and just say, 'Oh! That was yesterday....'"

6 chick corea

This is an expanded version of an article written for the May 2001 issue of *Piano*, celebrating Chick Corea's sixtieth birthday. It is based on our pre-concert talk (at which I interviewed him in front of an audience) for his November 1999 appearance at the Royal Festival Hall, and a long face-to-face interview at Yoshi's Jazz Club in Berkeley, California, the following year.

If ever there were a prize for musical polymaths, Chick Corea, who turns sixty on June 12, 2002, would certainly be on the shortlist. He's just won yet another Grammy for the instrumental arrangement of his most-requested composition *Spain*, and at the London concert in November 1999 where he and the London Philharmonic Orchestra premiered this version of the piece, plus a new arrangement of his own piano concerto, he also gave a sparkling rendition of Mozart's Piano Concerto No. 20 in D Minor (K466). After the concert he breezily announced that if the audience wanted to hear more, then he'd be playing jazz at Ronnie Scott's for the rest of the week. And as if that wasn't enough to pack into a few days, as soon as he'd finished in Soho, he set off on a world tour that took him as far afield as Stockholm and Osaka, during which he recorded his two magnificent solo albums released in 2001, *Standards* and *Originals*.

Corea's own piano concerto is unusual as such things go because unlike the Mozart, his own piano part is not entirely written, but includes several passages of improvisation, thereby bringing together the twin sides of his musical world, composition and jazz playing.

"Working with orchestras," says Corea, "the major attraction is actually the beautiful sound of the orchestra itself. My first experiences of playing with an orchestra were performing Mozart, which is all written notes. The extraordinary beauty and feeling of forty-plus musicians playing on stage is unique. It's not something that happens as part of the painter's art or the writer's art. It can get a little bit similar in a movie, say, but usually their crowd scenes are very artificially set up, whereas this is live with a huge group of people playing music together, and there's nothing else like it. The attraction of that experience made me want to develop new forms for it, and in doing so I came at it in a different direction from the way I normally work in a jazz context, which was firstly to write all the notes, so that the orchestra would feel comfortable, and then gradually to introduce sections of looseness and improvisation. Now, every time we perform my piano concerto, we find new ways to loosen it up. I think now that if I come to write a second piano concerto I'll try to introduce even more improvising elements from the outset, and maybe that'll include some for the orchestra."

Before leaving the subject of his orchestral collaborations, our conversation turns to his Grammy-winning arrangement of *Spain*. "I have times when I play the piece, and then I stop playing it for a while," he smiles, somewhat ruefully. "But then it's hard to deny the requests of audiences, as it's maybe the main one out of a small handful of pieces that my audience really remembers and asks for. So I thought this orchestral version would be the final hurrah, one last arrangement of *Spain*. If you listen to it you hear that the actual theme is embedded in ten minutes of new material at the front and another ten at the back that don't have a lot directly to do with it. But it was an attempt to present the theme again in a new setting."

Corea has enormous physical presence, and if you meet him face to face he gives the impression that were he to focus his mind to it there is nothing in music he couldn't achieve. Although he studied the piano formally from the age of four, his jazz playing took him away from the classics until he was well into his forties, but, undaunted, he then launched himself into a new phase of his extraordinary career, and released a recording of the Mozart concerto for two pianos in 1984. Soon afterwards, he began a collaboration with jazz-singer-turned-conductor Bobby McFerrin, eventually producing an album called *The Mozart Sessions* in 1996, which combines some fine classical playing with the jazz expertise of both men.

In his 1999 London concert, his approach to the Mozart No. 20 was a little unorthodox, and heads shook worriedly in the audience when instead of the expected orchestral introduction, he began with his own very contemporary-sounding cadenza. When I ask him why, his answer is both simple and practical: "It helps me relax, puts me directly in touch with the keyboard, and doesn't leave me sitting silently through the whole orchestral exposition before striking my first note."

He has always had extraordinary facility at the keyboard, and his five-CD set *Music Forever And Beyond* offers a glimpse of his childhood prowess with a charming recording of *I Don't See Me In Your Eyes Anymore*, cut when he was just eight years old. His Massachusetts child-

Chick Corea (left) with Gary Burton at a concert presented by the author for BBC Radio, 1997
(Derek Drescher)

hood brought him into contact with many jazz and Latin musicians, and percussionist Don Alias (who later played alongside Corea on records with Miles Davis) remembers his lively presence at many jam sessions in and around Boston in the early 1960s. The same decade, Corea began playing with many major jazz groups, notably for the now somewhat forgotten trumpeter Blue Mitchell. He made his own debut album, *Tones For Joan's Bones*, and ended up recording for Stan Getz, accompanying Sarah Vaughan, and then joining Miles Davis's quintet, in which he replaced Herbie Hancock.

In later years, he and Herbie formed a dazzling partnership at two pianos, and their duet concerts and albums are still talked about as masterly examples of unforced technique and sheer fun. The duo format seems to suit Chick particularly well, and I have always equally enjoyed his other long-term partnership, with vibraphonist Gary Burton, both in concert and on their many albums such as *Crystal Silence*. A high point of their collaboration was a concert on London's South Bank in late 1997, in which Chick played marimba alongside Burton's vibes in a splendid exploration of unusual tone colours. They also managed to explore some of Corea's favourite Latin rhythms with none of the usual trimmings of congas, scrapers and shakers.

"Gary and I have always managed to do at least one or two gigs a year," he reflects. "It's a musical relationship that has no end to it, and every time we get together, there's a spark that comes off from it. As a matter of fact we'll be together again during the three weeks this December [2001] when I'll be celebrating my sixtieth birthday with a residency at the Blue Note in New York. Gary's going to come down there and do some duets."

Back in 1970, Chick and bassist Dave Holland left Miles Davis at the same time, and went on to form a free jazz group called Circle, with Anthony Braxton and Barry Altschul. "We wanted to experiment, and try our best to delve completely into a world of improvised music," he recalls. "Every performance would have no preparation to it at all. No composition, no discussion, nothing. My tenure with Circle was pretty much the result of that experiment. We had a very, very fulfilling time, or at least I did anyway, with that approach. It's pretty wild to go out in front of an audience and not have anything prepared, as a group of three and then four musicians, and then create an evening of music. It was totally open, although the one thing we did work on was the mechanics of sound. But as far as the forms go, it was very open and left to anything that would happen."

Then, in 1971, Corea founded the band that brought him international fame in his own right, Return to Forever. "It was the complete reverse because there had come a point in Circle where I had begun to want to have a predictable effect, which means a rhythm, a song, a melody, a composition. I wanted to go back into composing again, so it was time for me to move on and do that, the result of which was forming my first Return to Forever band."

To start with, this was a gentle Latin-orientated group, with Brazilian singer Flora Purim and her husband, the percussionist Airto Moreira, at the core of its sound, but it gradually became a fully fledged rock fusion group. Gone was the airiness and grace of early albums such as *Light As A Feather* and in its place came the powerful guitar riffs of Bill Connors and thudding drumming of Lenny White. "I don't know how you get that effect that an electric guitarist gets when he wails on his instrument if it's at a very low level," says Chick. "That sound's about mass, the physical mass that comes at the audience, and you achieve that through volume. That's a key part of the experience, and I touched into it. For two, three, four years we did that in Return to Forever. We gained some things, undoubtedly, but we also lost some things, in terms of subtleties, harmonies and certain intimacies of music that I always enjoy."

The late 1970s led to a series of further rock-tinged albums packed with star guests, and it is a debatable point whether his growing interest in Scientology led Corea into the realms of fantasy in his titles and ideas, or whether it was responsible for the counter-current that saw him constantly straining to extend his abilities in new directions.

"I left that very high-powered sound for a while," he says. "Then I came back to it somewhat with the Elektric Band, although that was done in a more controlled way. Our balances were more like a balanced ensemble, with a good stage sound. Although the audience sound was loud, it was mixed very well. I made sure at that point to bring in good engineers as part of the group."

He has managed to juggle the different elements in his music very effectively over the last two decades, with a return to playing in acoustic settings, appearances as a soloist, in duos with Burton and Hancock, and most of all in a succession of trios and small jazz groups. His so-called "Akoustic Band," formed in the late 1980s with bassist John Patitucci and drummer Dave Weckl brought him firmly back into jazz territory, and he has seldom looked back since. His most impressive recent work has been with his current group Origin.

"The game with improvised music is always finding new ways to approach the material," observes Corea, as our conversation moves on to this band. "It's improvising with the process itself, trying to find a spontaneous way to make music happen so that it has that level of excitement which everyone likes. With Origin we just kept finding new ways to expand what was in the charts."

At the heart of this sextet (which most recently included British saxophonist Tim Garland), and largely responsible for the group's extremely high excitement quotient, is the close musical partnership of bassist Avishai Cohen and drummer Jeff Ballard. When I heard them at the Cheltenham Festival in 1999, the most distinctive thing about them was their rhythmic complexity. Corea will set up a whole series of polyrhythms, and then be joined by Cohen who hits and strums his bass from time to time to create a whole pattern of percussive effects, while Ballard effortlessly increases the rhythmic texture with every means at his disposal.

I suspect it is not just me who finds this musical partnership one of the most stimulating Corea has had in the last twenty years or so. Chick himself has obviously gone for it in a big way, and he will be celebrating his sixtieth birthday during the last leg of some extensive touring with what he calls his "New Trio." Yes, you've guessed it, the other members are Cohen and Ballard...

"Avishai, Jeff and myself have travelled together for some time with Origin, and we've played a lot of gigs as a band," says Chick. "It was a great three and a half years. What we decided to do next was not a matter of scaling down, but grew out of the fact that when the trio plays on its own, or when it's worked with me in my piano concerto, there's been something special about it. On the way back from an Origin tour, we did some gigs in Martinique, and the trio popped out as an entity on its own. We tried some new things, we improvised, and I ended up writing a couple of new pieces. It was so attractive and the format of a trio is so basic, such a classic formation, that it contains all the elements I like most as a musician. So I decided to try doing it even more. I wrote a few extra pieces, did a few more gigs with the trio and it just kept clicking so much I decided to make a project out of it."

Cohen and Ballard are both musicians whose careers he's encouraged not only in his groups, but also on his own Stretch record label, and I draw our conversation to a close by asking what he is aiming for in the label, in addition to providing a showcase for his own work.

"Everyone that's ever worked for me is essentially a creative artist in his own right, as composer, player, bandleader and so forth. For me, the game in the world of art culture is: the more the merrier. I want to change this idea of monopolization that the mass media has turned into. We've got such a great web of communication on the planet with the Internet, TV and radio, but it's been dominated by just a small number of items, especially in the art area. So I like the idea of helping other artists. And I think this is a factor that monitors the health of our culture, in terms of how many artists can be getting their message out, or getting their bands going. It just works for me to help these guys."

7 sylvie courvoisier

The boundaries between jazz and twentieth-century chamber music can be very blurry. There are moments on each of the two discs in Sylvie Courvoisier's double album *Abaton* where one becomes the other, or, at the very least, where a new common form seems to emerge. Courvoisier is doubly interesting in that she is a European musician who has chosen to make her way in America, yet without compromising the peculiarly European qualities that she brings to her music. This interview appeared in the November 2003 edition of *Piano*.

The idea of using classical compositions as a basis for jazz is not new. Most famously Jacques Loussier pioneered the genre in the 1950s with his original Play Bach Trio, and both Alec Templeton and George Shearing have tried it as well, along with jazz pianists such as John Lewis and Dave Brubeck. What marks out the Swiss-born pianist Sylvie Courvoisier as unusual is that instead of using the classical and romantic repertoire as her starting point, her work has strong connections to the twentieth-century chamber tradition.

Her new double CD *Abaton* features a trio that includes her husband, Mark Feldman, on the violin, along with the cellist Erik Friedlander, and each disc complements the other, the first consisting of four full-length compositions, and the second of nineteen short collective improvisations.

"It began when I received a commission from the city of Basle in 2000," she says. "It offered me freedom of choice as to whom I performed with, so I chose Mark and Erik. I wanted to write instrumental work that used the timbre of the classical piano trio, and at the time I had been listening a lot to chamber music by Schnittke and Shostakovich, so this was the sound I was after. I had already worked occasionally with Mark and Erik, and so I wrote the commission for them. Since then it's grown into a regular group."

Was it, I wonder, a trio that had the opportunity to play often?

"Yes, both in New York, where I'm based now, and in Europe. Also, we are currently working together as members of a larger twelve-piece ensemble, put together by John Zorn for what he calls his Cobra project, and it's interesting to see how our established way of playing as a trio fits with nine others, and, of course, how we integrate with John's rules for how this larger group will improvise. But when it's just the three of us, we play in settings that are unusual for a jazz or improvising ensemble. We don't like to use amplification, so this restricts us to small venues, halls of 500 seats or so, with an acoustic developed for classical performance. Of course, we do play in clubs and larger venues where we have to use amplification, but on the whole we prefer not to, and to interact acoustically."

Having mentioned that she was no longer based in Europe, what led her to leave Europe and settle in Brooklyn?

"I moved to the United States in 1998, and meeting Mark was part of the reason. But musically I was feeling pretty alone in Lausanne, where I'd studied and grown up. There weren't too many other people working in the areas of improvisation and new music. Before I left Switzerland, I played a couple of times in the States, and found a much more sympathetic environment there. At that stage the Tonic, in New York, hadn't opened, although it's since become very much a home for this

Sylvie Courvoisier (Deborah Feingold/ECM)

kind of music, but I was able to play at the Knitting Factory and one or two other clubs. And in Brooklyn I found a very good scene of similarly minded musicians, including the trumpeter Dave Douglas, saxophonist Tim Berne, drummer Jim Black, and a host of others, to the extent that we were able to do sessions in the neighbourhood."

I knew that Sylvie had made quite a reputation for herself as a soloist, but now it seems she mainly works in groups of one sort or another. She is quick to agree: "Yes, that's right. I used to play quite a lot as a soloist, and I still like to play solo, but I seem to have stopped doing so regularly some years ago. Actually right now I'm working on writing a set of piano studies that include windows for improvisation, and I expect to be playing these in concert during the coming year. They're pretty complicated, and it's going to be a challenge to see if these pieces hold the public's attention – or whether they're too abstract!"

It seems to me that she has used this same technique of introducing what she calls "windows" for improvisation in some of the compositions on her new disc.

"True," she says, "but these aren't exactly what jazz musicians tend to call 'blowing sections,' where they play straightforward improvisations. Maybe the closest to that comes in the title track, *Abaton* itself, where there's quite a rhythmical groove pattern going on, and Mark plays a solo that draws on the kind of much more straightforward jazz he's been doing with John Abercrombie or Dave Douglas's groups. Erik has worked in other groups, too, and I'm sure he brings something of that experience into the trio, but I think what we've tried to achieve is a means of improvising that's very close to the sound of my compositions. In fact, it's that closeness that led to the new disc becoming a double album. Originally, Manfred Eicher at ECM was just going to record my four compositions for a disc in his New Series. But we finished recording them quite quickly, and he suggested we use up the extra studio time by recording some improvisations, which is what we did, and the two seemed to complement each other. At one point we thought of interleaving the short improvisations between the compositions, but in the end we put them on a separate disc, and they have a unity of their own."

How does she see the balance between being an improvising pianist and a composer in her work overall?

"The writing definitely came first, when I was as young as ten or eleven. I've always written, although I am self-taught as a composer. I actually tend to be a little shy about what I've done – maybe because I didn't study like everybody else, I'm not really able to talk about it. That's part of my character. I'd rather play music than talk about it!"

8 tommy flanagan

This birthday tribute to Tommy Flanagan appeared in the May 2000 issue of *Piano*. He seemed on good form, was still issuing albums and appearing regularly around New York. So his death in November 2001 was something of a shock, and it seemed impossible that we would no longer see him sitting with his imperturbable upright posture at the keys, or hear his calm mastery of almost all styles of jazz, which I'd initially witnessed at first hand in 1976.

Tommy Flanagan turned seventy in March 2000, and at first sight he's nowadays a rather willowy, slender figure, but there's nothing willowy or slender about his piano playing. As his most recent album from the Village Vanguard demonstrates, he's still got all the power, imagination and drive that made him the pianist of choice for everyone from Miles Davis and John Coltrane to Sonny Rollins and Ella Fitzgerald.

On the Vanguard disc, Lewis Nash is the latest in a long line of drummers who have worked in Tommy's trios over the years, from Bobby Durham and Ed Thigpen back to illustrious modern jazz pioneers such as Roy Haynes. But perhaps his most enduring musical relationship is with Elvin Jones, who comes from the same home town: "Elvin and I started playing in Detroit at a club called the Bluebird," he recalled, "which was a kind of a legendary landmark because it's where all the great musicians used to come through town, like Charlie Parker, for example. They'd usually come as a guest, or sit in with our local group. I played there with Miles Davis for about three months, and then later on with saxophonist Wardell Gray and trumpeter Clifford Brown.

"Some of these players just stopped by to listen because the house band was pretty good, with Thad Jones, Billy Mitchell, Elvin, myself and bassist James Richardson, whose brother Rodney played with Count Basie. The band was together a long time, perhaps five years because when I went in the army I got my gig with them back again when I came out!"

Tommy Flanagan (Redferns)

I wondered if this early experience had helped Tommy's ability to lock on to Elvin Jones's sense of time, apparently having no difficulty in handling Jones's tendency to play against the beat, or complex counter-rhythms: "I think we've got something special going there because you're right, he does change things around quite a bit. Many of the young drummers who try to play like him end up getting lost, just as some older players tell me they have trouble hearing the 'one' – the downbeat in every bar – although it's always there in Elvin's playing. You can't always feel it, you have to pay attention when you're exchanging four or eight bars, and he's even caught me napping a couple of times. The one guy who never gets lost with him is his brother Hank. He always had the knack of knowing where Elvin was all the time."

Mention of Hank Jones reminds me of the 1978 album *Our Delights* that he and Tommy had recorded together. "I haven't done too much with two pianos, and I was very happy about that because Hank was a kind of early influence on me. People think I heard Hank in Detroit, but I didn't. I first heard him live a year or two after I got to New York in the mid-1950s, and a little later on I thought perhaps I could get some tutoring from him. So I went up to him between sets and asked him if he had any time to show me a few things. He turned to me and said: 'Tommy, I've got all your records.'

"That just about blew me away, and so I said in that case I didn't think I'd bother him!"

I wondered if this interest in Hank Jones had anything to do with the fact that they were both ideal accompanists for Ella Fitzgerald, both spending several years in her touring groups. In particular, it seemed to me they both had the ability to create the right kind of space for her vocals. "I think she demanded that," said Tommy. "And I used Hank as a model for how to accompany – instrumentalists as well as singers – and not just his playing, but his whole manner. He can seem to be quite hard to approach, very formal, until you get to know him, that is, when the Jones side of him comes out."

I first heard Tommy with Ella and the Count Basie Orchestra, in one of a series of concerts where Tommy and his trio would take over as the band's rhythm section for Ella's final set. Clearly Tommy loved this experience, his eyes lighting up at the memory of their extensive tours; but, he remembered: "Sometimes we'd come to the end of a three-week season with the Basie band, and Ella's trio would go back to doing our own gigs. And halfway through the first set, Ella would turn to me without fail and say, 'Tommy, what's missing?'

"And I'd say: 'Oh, about fifteen men, that's all!' But she was great to tour with, a great big band singer, and of course she'd improvise like an instrumentalist, you know."

Tommy's many albums with Ella, with whom he worked as accompanist in 1956, from 1963–65 and again from 1968–78, all demonstrate his extraordinary sensitivity as a supporting player. And, although his impressive stream of discs as a soloist, or leading his own trio, prove he's no slouch at taking the spotlight himself, his other most impressive achievement is appearing as pianist on two of the greatest jazz albums of all time, Sonny Rollins's *Saxophone Colossus* and John Coltrane's *Giant Steps*.

While acknowledging that, Tommy was quick to point out that he was also accompanist, in clubs and on record for another great tenorist, Coleman Hawkins, which was quite a skill in its own right, and made even more so when Hawk was joined by other combative improvisers such as Roy Eldridge and Johnny Hodges, for example on their Verve album *Hawkins! Eldridge! Hodges! Alive!* from the Village Gate. I knew that Tommy got to work with Coltrane because they were neighbours, but how had this young lion of the bebop movement ended up with a swing-era giant such as Hawkins? The answer came with a conspiratorial wink: "I think he had a fondness for pianists from Detroit!"

9 michael garrick

Written for the May 2003 *Jazzwise*, this interview celebrated the seventieth birthday of one of Britain's most prolific and imaginative jazz musicians, whose work deserves to be far more widely known than it is. Michael Garrick's music had a big influence on me as a boy, as he not only worked in and around Camberley, Surrey, which was not far from where I grew up, but I also knew several of the Farnborough-based choristers who sang in his big liturgical works. His sextet gave me my first chance to hear musicians such as Ian Carr, Don Rendell, Art Themen and John Marshall in the flesh, and I heard them all in the days before the ground-breaking Rendell-Carr Quintet (in which Michael was the pianist) broke up. In either configuration, this was among Britain's most forward-looking jazz of its time, and in the three decades or so since then, Michael has never abandoned that lonely position ahead of the pack. I have supplemented the original article with parts of a later interview which appeared in the March 2004 edition of *Piano*.

When Michael Garrick turns seventy, he'll already have had the satisfaction of celebrating in style with a birthday concert at London's Queen Elizabeth Hall, which featured his big band plus special guests Don Rendell and Anita Wardell. The concert itself drew on music from all stages of Garrick's busy and energetic career, from his pioneering 1960s work with the Rendell-Carr Quintet to his long-term partnership with Joe Harriott, not to mention his long involvement with poetry (and in a wider sense, the spoken or sung word) and jazz.

But when we met in the quiet corner of Berkhamsted where he lives, we quickly moved on to another of his achievements, *Jazz Praises*, which he had worked into the concert in a rather different way.

"I'd intended to open the second half with my current quartet," he said, "but when it came down to it, there really wasn't time. As the focus of the whole event was the big band, I decided to do something from *Jazz Praises* because although it was originally written for sextet and choir, I've now reworked a lot of it for the larger forces of the big band. I chose the section called *Behold A Pale Horse*, from the Book of Revelations, and there were two reasons for this. The first was that I had a rather good recording of the original performance in St Paul's Cathedral from 1968 – I'd even gone out and bought a stereo machine in honour of the occasion, but I only had one microphone, so it ended up in mono – and I'd played the introduction to this section on the organ as a sort of Hammer horror piece.

"During the period leading up to that premiere, I'd been able to get into St Paul's at night because the organist, Christopher Dearnley, was a jolly good sort, and he agreed to let me in at any time when the cathedral was closed. So I had the wonderful experience of going into that building by myself, and playing all night if I wanted to. Because of that I was able to take my time to discover the range of sounds on the instrument, which is a truly magnificent Henry Willis organ with five separate manuals. For this introduction to *Pale Horse*, I worked out how to use its extremes, ranging from the very tiny celestial sounds of the little pipes hidden away behind the altar, to the massive dome tubas which made a great honking noise. What I was trying to express was the opening of hell, from which the pale horse of death was going to trot out.

"I found a 32-foot bombard stop, and I put both feet sideways on the pedals so I got the very lowest notes of all in a huge cluster. It was such an incredible noise with all these huge pipes growling together that I thought I'd damage the building if I kept it up. Well, the building survived, and I made the recording – including this huge sound. So why is that important? A couple of years later, Christopher Dearnley asked me to do a lunchtime recital on the organ, and by that stage the console had been moved and the organ partially rebuilt. I looked for the 32-foot bombard, and it had gone. What that means is there's no more opportunity to hear that extraordinary bass register, so this recording of mine captured something irreplaceable, which is why I used it to start the second half of the concert. There was no announcement, just this thunderous volcanic sound, then it died down, and I conducted the band into the body of the piece.

"Which brings me to the second reason for doing *Pale Horse*, namely Ian Carr's flugelhorn solo from the original concert. I listened to it quite recently, and thought, 'I wonder how it would sound if I took down Ian's solo from the record and orchestrated it?' Consequently I did just that, and it worked, although I never told Ian about it. Then, not long before the concert, I happened to see Ian and I told him if he came to the concert he'd have a surprise. He came along, and there was his solo, played by the whole orchestra, which proves better than anything that jazz improvisation is real composition. You hear it, notate it, orchestrate it, and there you are – a demonstration that the soloist produced a lovely piece of music on the spot. And I wanted to do this for Ian in gratitude for all the music we've made together."

The 1960s Rendell-Carr Quintet discs on which both Ian and Michael appear are well-known if [until their 2004 reissue by BGO Records] hard to find, but less familiar today are the records from the same period made by Garrick's own groups, in which Carr alternated with Shake Keane as the main trumpeter.

After Ian moved on from his sextet and formed Nucleus, Michael continued to use musicians who were not only personalities that fitted and extended his music, but who tended to be either up-and-coming or established but not-so-well-known players. First, there was the much under-rated tenorist Jim Philip, and then in the 1970s the combination of the young, hirsute Henry Lowther (on trumpet and violin) and the ethereal voice of Norma Winstone.

"As a soloist, you never know what you can do until you're put on the spot and asked to do it," said Michael. "It's happened to a lot of people, where I've suggested they play something, and they've mumbled a bit about 'Don't know about that...,' before giving it a try. It's about finding really good musicians with an open attitude, and this has led to some very interesting results. These days, I think there are fewer and fewer instrumentalists who want to stay in one place and not move on, but back in the sixties and seventies I was always happy to find open-minded players."

The major platform for this extension of the stylistic range of his players has been Garrick's large-scale compositions. And there have been plenty of them: suites based on J. R. R. Tolkein, on Thomas Hardy, and on Lewis Carroll, as well as the more devotional pieces such as *Jazz Praises*, *Mr Smith's Apocalypse* and *Bovingdon Poppies*. Only Mike Westbrook – a man similarly devoted to Ellingtonian big band ideas – has been so consistently prolific among British jazz composers at creating works with comparable scope. So what's the attraction?

"I'm just interested in these subjects. Once I get started, the pieces just grow. In most cases it's like having a house-plant that, before you know it, needs to be replanted in the garden. It was exactly like that with the first one, *Jazz Praises*. I never set out to write a series of pieces. I wrote a tune that was processional, in four-part harmony, and I followed my nose, put it away for a bit, brought it out, worked on it, and it became some wedding music. Actually, the Modern Jazz Quartet

[MJQ] was an influence – the way they'd start with a contrapuntal section, a pastiche of Bach, and then suddenly you'd have these fantastic swinging solos, before going back to the Bach again. That appealed to me, not least because all my life I felt I was constantly having to prove to my parents, my teachers, everyone like that, that 'jazz is music.' I think that's stayed with me for far too long, although I keep meeting people now who seem to have that same disapproving attitude, and I constantly want to show them that jazz should be taken as seriously as any other form of music."

This desire to make a point means that several of Garrick's largest, most wide-ranging pieces have been entirely self-motivated. But there were commissions, too. *Mr Smith's Apocalypse* began life at the 1969 Farnham Festival as a *Jazz Requiem For Martin Luther King*. And then twenty years later, Dick Teague, from Dorchester, asked Michael to write a piece for the 150th anniversary of Thomas Hardy's birth, with a concert in the town's Eldridge Pope Maltings concert hall. It was to become one of his most successful and emotionally charged works.

"He sent me a few titles – lines out of the novels, which he thought might inspire compositions. They were lovely names for pieces; things like *Blue As An Autumn Mist* or *Meteors Close At Hand*. At this stage, although I'd studied *The Mayor of Casterbridge* at school, I didn't feel the need to go and read all the rest of the books – I got off on the titles, and soon there were six pieces written to start the whole process. But he'd sent me twelve or so lines from Hardy, and I kept picking up another one and thinking, 'I can do something with this.' Worse still, I started writing words to some of them, and so I had to call Norma Winstone in to sing them at the premiere of what became *Hardy Country*, along with the quartet of Jimmy Hastings, Dave Green, Alan Jackson and myself, for whom they were originally commissioned. I also set a couple of poems of Hardy's for good measure.

"After the event, I thought about how I might expand some of them into a big band format, and I ended up doing exactly that and recording several for the album *Meteors Close At Hand* in 1994. That demonstrates how an idea takes on a kind of organic growth in my work."

To me the principal characteristic of *Hardy Country*, like a lot of Garrick's jazz, is its Englishness. A case in point is his recent disc, *Green And Pleasant Land*, which includes an atmospheric piece about the Oxfordshire village of Bladon. How does he feel about the observation that his music is quintessentially English?

"It's me. It's who I am. It's something I realized while I was still at University in London in the late 1950s, reading English literature, and playing in various West End clubs at the same time. I started out doing boogie woogie, or transcriptions of George Shearing, which you could buy back then, and I remember wondering what hope had this little white kid from Enfield got of being like Earl Hines or Fats Waller? At the same time the critics were all talking about roots. Benny Green was fulminating against the MJQ and Brubeck for taking jazz away from its black working-class roots and into the concert hall. I realized there was all this other culture in England that's got nothing to do with Harlem, but is very rich, especially in literature. And so I investigated the English folk-song tradition – *Barbara Allen*, *Raggle Taggle Gipsies*, *Greensleeves* – doing arrangements of these and featuring them on my very first quartet record, with Pete Shade on vibes. In fact Denis Preston didn't issue the session at the time, and some years later Alistair Robertson at Hep brought it out on an LP called *Chronos*, but it gives an insight into how I was already using these very English ideas as a basis for jazz.

"Pete Shade knew of a club where we could play an interval set, called El Toro, which was on the Finchley Road, and run by Peter Burman, who came up after hearing us and said how much he'd enjoyed this 'English stuff.' He was involved in some way or another with the National Jazz Federation [NJF], who were in the process of opening the original Marquee Club on Oxford Street, and Peter got us in to play the opening night opposite Kenny Baker. What we were doing went over marvellously. In some ways we were very, very amateur, but we were novel because nobody else was using British themes in their jazz.

"Consequently, we stayed at the Marquee for months, and that's how I met Joe Harriott because Kenny Baker only played on the opening night, and after that, for the NJF's weekly session, Joe Harriott's quintet became the main band, and we were the support."

Before we got round to the subject of Harriott, I wanted to pick up on the literary side of Garrick's exploration of his roots. Since the 1960s, he's always had an affinity for literature, something he shares with a number of his contemporaries: Ian Carr, for example, has done settings of Shakespeare; Stan Tracey has set Dylan Thomas; and Mike Westbrook has set William Blake. But whereas Garrick has also written settings of material from the literary canon, he's always been equally involved in contemporary literature, going right back to the days of his 1960s Poetry and Jazz concerts on the South Bank.

"It began when I found a copy of James Weldon Johnson's *God's Trombones* lying on the floor in Dillons, and after a minute or two's browsing, I knew it had to have some jazz to go with it, so I wrote a piece which we played in the old recital room at the Royal Festival Hall. A chap called

Jeremy Robson heard it, and he got us involved in a series of concerts for the trade union movement organized by Arnold Wesker. My quartet with Shake Keane on trumpet played what eventually became the Poetry and Jazz package alongside poets like Dannie Abse, Adrian Mitchell and Laurie Lee. In due course, we expanded into a quintet with Joe Harriott joining the line-up. After listening to contemporary poets reading their work, we would improvise our own versions of the poems, so that the literary side of my interests became real, through working, hanging out and, just as importantly, having a laugh with all the great writers of the day. When Shake went to Germany in 1965, I carried on doing these concerts with members of the Rendell-Carr group because firstly Ian took over Shake's role in responding spontaneously to the poetry, and then Don eventually came in to replace Joe, who was becoming harder to pin down."

Despite this connection with contemporary poetry, Michael's most recent literature-related work is his personal response to one of the best-loved children's plays in the English language. In December 1992, I was at the Vortex jazz club in Stoke Newington, listening to one of the regular monthly sessions by his big band, when amid pieces by Duke Ellington and Billy Strayhorn, well-known and not-so-well-known, they suddenly went into a gentle, delicate ballad, full, as I wrote at the time, of "shimmering flutes and clarinets, muted brass, and [a] sweet orchestration." The tune was *Wendy* from Garrick's jazz dance suite *Peter Pan*, a lengthy work that the band has subsequently got round to recording in its entirety.

The *Peter Pan Suite* was first performed in the context of one of Garrick's educational concerts, at Beechwood School, Tunbridge Wells, and the liner notes for the album include a painting by the junior department there, complete with Peter, Wendy, the Darlings, the Lost Boys, Hook and his Crocodile: all in all a mixture of vibrant images stimulated by the listening experience of hearing Garrick's interpretation of the story.

"The majority of children we play for are in the junior or middle school range," said Garrick, "and that's been the case since the 1960s, when I began working in schools in Hampshire in a collaboration with Victor Fox, a most enlightened figure who was the music inspector in the local authority, who later moved to Manchester and carried on very similar work. My motive has always been to give some idea of the joy and fun to be found in music, and I've found it's appreciated from the youngest nursery school age on upwards. At the higher end, I've written for secondary choirs and ensembles, with my largest scale piece of all, *Zodiac Of Angels*, being scored for the Manchester Youth Orchestra, full choir, solo voice and jazz group, plus dancers. But whatever the age level, part of the secret is to have respect for enquiring minds, and never to dumb down."

Michael Garrick at the Royal Academy of Music, 1991 (Derek Drescher)

Maybe Michael's so evangelical about this because his own school experiences were exactly the opposite, in what he refers to as "the indelibly non-inspirational town" of Enfield, where his efforts to play jazz were met with "ridicule, petty-mindedness and complacency." He's been a leading light in advocating the new Associated Board jazz examinations, and much of his motivation comes from his periods of teaching at the Royal Academy of Music or Trinity College. "I'd see students come in who were well-trained classical musicians, who had absolutely no idea what a C seventh chord was. And even those who had some inkling of how to play jazz would look completely blank when major figures like Duke Ellington or Charlie Parker were mentioned. So my rationale is that since every young musician in Britain tends to work through the Associated Board grades on their instrument, jazz ought to be incorporated as an option alongside the other material they play."

With the first exams now in place, it's the end of a long crusade which began in the 1980s, when Garrick first set out the case. Yet his persistence is equally long-term when it comes to composition. You don't dash off large-scale multi-movement suites in an instant, and Garrick still loves the monthly opportunity of his Vortex sessions (destined to be homeless when redevelopment finally prompts the long-expected closure of the club) to hear his music being played by his big band as works in progress. It's also an opportunity for the symbiotic relationship between words and music to develop, a case in point being *Peter Pan* where, as Garrick says, "there was no original intention to have words, they just began arriving by brain-fax...we decided on a combination of solo and choral speech and song."

In the early days of Michael's career, Joe Harriott and Shake Keane were both equally closely involved in creating similar links between poetry and jazz, sharing the evolution of the music and words. Talk of Joe brings us to the fact that Michael's seventieth birthday falls in the thirtieth year since Joe's death from cancer, aged just forty-four. In his memory, Michael dubbed 2003 "The Year of the Harriott," and the Garrick Quintet with Martin Hathaway and Steve Waterman aims to do its bit to commemorate Joe's music. One area of Garrick's common ground with Joe was their shared interest in Indian music. While Joe co-led Indo-Jazz Fusions with violinist John Mayer, Michael chose to explore Indian ideas in the compositions he write for Harriott and for Rendell-Carr, such as *Voices*, using the scale of C as a raga, and *Heart Is A Lotus* in 11/4 time. "This was just one aspect of ideas we both explored. So little's been done to recognize Joe's crucial importance to European jazz. I hope that in time more people will come to realize the extraordinary richness of his legacy."

10 benny green

In 2000, I was involved in making a BBC television film about the Brecon Jazz festival in Wales, which looked at the event through the eyes of various participants, including a painter, a critic and a musician. I was the critic, Benny Green was the musician, and the resulting documentary *My Brecon* drew our respective stories together. By that time I had already got to know Benny, and have always subsequently tried to make a point of hearing him on his British visits. This interview was written for the January 2001 edition of *Piano*.

It's been a tough few days for Benny Green. He's been up in Oregon, playing in a trio with bassist Ray Brown, and he has just a day or so at home in New York before he has to take off again. But being Benny, he relaxes by listening back to a recording of last night's session with Ray Brown, enthusing over the bassist's prowess, and, as the piano comes in, being his own sternest critic. I've made my way to his Manhattan apartment to talk to him for a BBC documentary about his mentor Oscar Peterson, but once we've finished our official work, we sit back and talk about Benny's own career.

He's just moved from the Blue Note record label to Telarc, and his album *Naturally* has just been released a day or two before we meet. For the most part it's a trio with guitarist Russell Malone and bassist Christian McBride, two of Benny's old friends who toured with him in 1999 and again briefly last summer. But, for me, the real interest in this disc lies in Benny's three solo tracks: the slow, elegant stride of Ellington's *Love You Madly*, the wistful Wayne Shorter tune *Lester Left Town*, and the highlight, a brief, intense version of a song called *Learnin' The Blues*.

Anyone who has seen Benny on his recent British tours (and he worked in the UK a lot in 1998–99) will know that his precise, positive touch is getting more and more individual and distinctive as he matures, but on these solos there is still, I think, more than a hint of Oscar Peterson. So how had he fallen under the Peterson influence?

"I met Oscar in the fall of 1992, in Toronto, where I was playing with Ray Brown, and Ray invited him to hear a show. I met him before we went on, and it was a thrill just to shake the giant hand that had affected me for so long. I was extremely self-conscious playing in front of him for the first time, so I went and hid in the dressing room when we came off. Then I realized he'd been so warm to me beforehand, that whatever I felt about what I'd played, on a human level I ought to go back out there and spend time with him. So I went to his table, and he said, 'Benny, it's a pleasure to hear the piano played the way I like to hear it played!'

"He pretty much opened up to me from then on, and we began communicating by telephone and mail, and at the beginning of 1993 he called me one day while I was practising. Normally, I don't pick up the phone when I'm working at the piano, but I heard his voice on my answering machine, and I grabbed the receiver. He told me he'd been chosen to receive the Glenn Gould award for excellence in music in Toronto, and the recipient had to designate a protégé – someone he saw as representing the kind of qualities he believed in or stood for. He said he'd chosen me, which was an incredible surprise.

"I travelled up there for a ceremony that entailed performing some of his pieces and playing duets with him. But the influence and inspiration

Benny Green at the Brecon Jazz Festival, 1997 (Derek Drescher)

he's given me was vast, much bigger and wider than our direct connection through this award. I can still spend entire days listening to his recordings, and whereas listening to most pianists palls after a few hours, I never find I get tired of his work. I think I can transform my experience as a listener by trying to bring the kind of qualities I enjoy in his playing into mine. They're intangible qualities you can't define, or write out on manuscript paper."

When Benny mentions his duets with Oscar, I remember that a few years back he made a duo album with Oscar, a privilege only previously afforded to Count Basie.

"That was a glimpse into a kind of Norman Granz way of running a record date, something I'd experienced with Ray Brown as well. For one thing there were never more than two takes recorded of a song, and the second was done begrudgingly and only in cases of absolute necessity. So if you're going to make any kind of classic statement, you have to get it done immediately. I guess that's how things were back in the fifties. But I learned a real lesson from Oscar on that date. He overheard me making a side comment to the engineer that the piano I was playing was giving me a bit of a problem with a very resistant action. I'd never have said this directly to him, but he came over and asked if I was having trouble. Then he suggested we trade pianos, and the more I backed down, the more insistent he became, and so we traded instruments.

"I sat at the one he'd been playing and we rolled the tapes. Oscar played the piano I'd been using so beautifully that in his hands there appeared to be nothing wrong with it. After we finished I turned to him and said, 'I see it's the player not the piano.' But later on, I was talking to the producer who said that Oscar had said afterwards: 'That'll be a good lesson for him!' And I've never complained about an instrument since that day."

We then go off into a digression about all the bad pianos we've each encountered, and how Art Tatum had played some of his greatest sessions on some of the worst instruments. And that brings us back, finally, to Benny's current trio which is modelled on the Tatum trio's instrumentation, although that's where the resemblance stops.

"I wrote tunes with the specific musical voices of Russell and Christian in mind," says Benny. "If you have someone in your band you enjoy playing with, you can receive ideas from their musical personality. At the same time I'm careful with the direction of the band, so my compositions don't lose the adventure and drama that comes from improvisation."

11 herbie hancock

The main conversation here is one prompted by the release of Herbie's 2001 album, *Future 2 Future*, and which was published in that October's *Jazzwise*. But as a preamble, I have included another part of the same interview which concerns his early career. It appeared in the following month's *Piano* magazine.

There's a moment at the end of Herbie Hancock's recent Verve album, *Gershwin's World*, when he casts aside electronics and fellow musicians alike, and produces a shimmering, translucently beautiful solo version of *Embraceable You*. For all his chart successes with discs such as *Rockit* in the 1980s, and the hard-hitting funk of his earlier Head Hunters band, Hancock remains one of the most supremely gifted solo pianists in jazz. When we spoke recently, he was only too happy to look back at his early days in New York, and the steps that led him to become one of the leading players on the Blue Note label in the 1960s.

The young Chicagoan had recently arrived in New York, and was playing with trumpeter Donald Byrd, with whom he shared a Bronx apartment. After a freelance session in which he and Byrd appeared on a Pepper Adams disc, Herbie made his first two Blue Note albums in the autumn of 1961 as a member of Byrd's regular quintet.

"When I first started recording," Herbie remembered, "I hadn't a clue about the business. So I was absolutely lucky to begin working with Alfred Lion at Blue Note. When I came on the scene, this was the hottest label for new music, although because Alfred and his partner Frank Wolff were running a successful business, it had an inbuilt element of conservatism. They were always cautious about recording new people. It was a kind of chicken and egg situation: they'd record you if they knew you, but how were they going to get to know you, if you hadn't had the chance to record? Other musicians of my age who began to make their own discs did so because they'd been introduced to the inner circle. Wayner Shorter and Lee Morgan, for example, were there because of Art Blakey. Horace Silver was a little bit older than me, and he'd been around New York for a while. And all of them were making records. So it was marvellous for me that Donald got me on the label."

Recording with Byrd was one thing, even though the band was a stellar collection of musicians including saxophonist Wayne Shorter and drummer Billy Higgins, but I wondered how Herbie had made the much more difficult jump to making albums under his own name.

"That was down to Donald. One day, while we were sharing that apartment in the Bronx, he just said to me, 'It's time for you to make a record.' He was like a big brother figure to me, but even so I said, 'No! No! I'm not ready.' But he was persuasive. He said, 'Here's what you do. Tell them you got drafted, and you want to make a record before you go in the army.' So that's what I did.

"In those days, they'd usually create an album by allowing you to do three of your own pieces, but the rest was made up with three standards that the buying public would recognize. It was as if you were doing three for the company and three for yourself. So, I thought to myself, I should have a go at writing a piece that would actually become a standard, a piece that would help to sell the record. I asked myself what kind of thing was actually selling, and I figured if I did straightahead jazz pieces as the three standards, I could do something a little different as the 'commercial' piece. So I began putting *Watermelon Man* together. I figured that the funky sound was popular at the time, so I should come up with something funky, but at the same time, I wanted the tune to have something 'real' about it, to reflect some part of the African-American experience. So I tried to capture a real-life character, the man who had his horse and cart going through the streets of Chicago, selling watermelons. I wanted the rhythm to reflect the idea of wagon wheels on the cobblestones, echoing in the alleys of Chicago, and the melody came from the women leaning out of their windows and shouting out 'Hey! Watermelon Man!'

"So I brought that and three other pieces to Alfred. I told him I'd balance up the disc with a blues and some standards, but he said, 'No! I want three more originals.' Now that was really unusual because they *never* had entirely original pieces on an artist's first album. But I guess when he heard *Watermelon Man* he heard dollar signs! Now Donald had told me the next thing Alfred would try and do was put the copyrights in his own Blue Note publishing company. Donald said, 'Tell them, no, that you've published it yourself.' I turned to him and said, 'But they might not let me do the record.' But he nodded, 'Trust me, they will!'

"So, OK, I did exactly as he said. I said, 'Sorry, no, I can't publish it with you, I've already published it with my own company.' And so Alfred looked at the floor and said, 'Well, I guess we can't go ahead with the record.'

"I turned to walk out, and just as my hand hit the doorknob, Alfred said, 'Hang on! I think we'll make the record after all.'"

And, as it turned out, the single of *Watermelon Man*, from Herbie's first album, *Takin' Off*, hit the charts, and became an even bigger hit when Mongo Santamaria cut a cover version a few months later. And with that disc, made forty years ago [in 1962], the unstoppable career of Herbie Hancock as one of jazz's major pianists and composers got well and truly under way.

> With that background established, the timescale shifts forward to the present, and the other part of our conversation, as it appeared in *Jazzwise*.

Whenever I've talked to Herbie Hancock for any length of time, it's not long before we get onto the subject of gadgets. More than any musician I can think of, Herbie just loves technology, new bits of kit that do things you couldn't do before, or where a piece of electronic wizardry becomes a seamless part of the creative process. When we hooked up to talk about his new album *Future 2 Future*, which sees him reunited with another master of technology, producer, bassist and editor extraordinaire Bill Las-

Herbie Hancock during an interview with the author,
Dorchester Hotel, London, 1997 (Derek Drescher)

well, it took us a while to get round to the disc itself because Herbie was still full of the excitement of using a surround-sound PA system on the tour he'd just finished in July [2001].

The band on that tour had been pretty impressive in its own right – Wallace Roney on trumpet, Matthew Garrison (son of Jimmy) on bass, Terri Lyne Carrington on drums and, doubling up alongside Herbie himself on keyboards and sequencer, Darryl Diaz – but what really got Herbie excited was that on his seven Italian concerts he had tried out a new six-channel mixing system intended to give every seat in the house a comparable balance, recreating the immediacy of sound that the musicians themselves could hear from within the group. And that's not all. When he goes out again on the road in November, for a tour that will take in a higher proportion of clubs and small venues than usual, Herbie plans not only to use a further refined version of the sound system, but to add visuals and projected images.

He had launched off into an enthusiastic description of the capabilities of a new Macintosh program he plans to use called G-Force that can modify projected images in response to musical cues, when I gently suggested that we might return to the subject of his new disc – not least because it, too, has its technological dimension.

In the early 1980s, during his last great collaboration with Bill Laswell, which produced *Future Shock*, *Perfect Machine* and *Sound System*, digital editing technology was in its infancy, and Laswell went to some lengths to create the final results, particularly on the hit single *Rockit*, even though, once all the elements were assembled, the final issued mix was knocked out in about an hour and a half. The steps that led to that mix involved feeding Daniel Ponc's *bata* playing, the turntable work of Grand Mixer DST, and Laswell's own basslines (derived from Pharoah Sanders's tune *Tahaud*) into a sequencer, but leaving the music space to breathe, and for Herbie to add his own inimitable ingredients to the end result.

"Now," said Herbie, "all that has become far, far easier. Technology is on such a different level today that sampling, cut-and-paste, even the recording process itself, are almost as easy as word-processing. I really enjoy working with Bill because his scope is so broad, and in the middle of this technological environment he retains a spontaneous element. I think what happened when we got back together was that we both wanted to open up to using those technical possibilities as much as possible. But at the same time we agreed there would be one key element we wanted to preserve from our earlier work, which is that neither of us wanted to produce a 'thinking' record; we wanted something that was more right side of the brain: spontaneous, reactive, inspirational."

To a large extent, despite the constraints of a repetitive rhythmic format, they have been successful in capturing that kind of spontaneity, and Herbie puts this down to two things: firstly the working methods that he and Laswell have evolved, and secondly the way that the musical climate itself has changed in the fifteen years or so since they were last in the studio together.

"Bill prepares the elements of each piece," said Herbie. "Then he brings them to me. Take the one that features DJ Rob Swift for example. Bill had laid down a bass part and a drum part, and he had recorded Rob Swift's own parts, but he had them all on different tracks, so what I heard when he brought it to me was not necessarily in the form of the final result. All the elements were there, and he set to work to create the form for the piece after I had put my ideas on, including an electric piano solo. Once I'd added my couple of things and suggested places where there might be a nice recurring element, then he produced the end result. But there is a change in our musical thinking, mainly to do with the way we used to be concerned about everything fitting together so perfectly. That's where there's been the biggest move forward since the eighties. Newer hip-hop music doesn't come from where I came from, that's to say music with European rules, with a traditional harmonic sense and neat four- or eight-bar phrases. Today's players just don't think in those terms, so what you'll find on the record is an area that lies somewhere between my kind of harmonic background and a kind of naïve lack of harmonic sense."

Talking about Laswell's methodology immediately put me in mind of his posthumous re-editing of Miles Davis material on the *Panthalassa* album, especially his daring reinterpretation of *In A Silent Way*, using material that Miles and his producer Teo Macero had left on the cutting-room floor. When I asked Herbie about this, he laughed his gigantic laugh, and said: "Well, to tell you the truth, one of the pieces on the new disc was put together from out-takes, or different elements that had not eventually been used in some of the other numbers. I'm not going to tell you which track, but you might spot it because it has a drum 'n' bass pattern that's repeated from time to time, and which Bill has used almost like a chorus."

As this effect is used more than once on the disc, I'm still not sure which track this is, and Herbie wasn't telling, but he did pick up on another area of my comparison with *Panthalassa*. "In making *Future 2 Future*, and I guess our earlier discs too, Bill was less of a producer than a producer/musician. And, yes, you're right. It is kind of analogous to Teo Macero and what he did with Miles, from the standpoint of putting the album together after the fact. Teo was the first person I knew who did that. But I think Bill's role is much more integral – the entire construction of the new album is Bill's own; he has a vision before we start work on a piece. But with Miles, we'd arrive at the studio and there'd just be elements, like two or three bars, and he'd say 'Play that!' We'd wind up going from that tiny fragment to a full day of music, but when the time came to leave the studio, and the door shut behind us, we wouldn't know what the heck we'd got. Teo would take the tapes away and later he'd make a piece."

Laswell's skills at creating musical collage have developed a long way since *Future Shock*, but I wondered, when it came to the new collaboration, how Herbie had kept pace with the changes in the quasi-underground scene that Laswell inhabits. Back in 1983, when they were making *Rockit* together, Laswell had coaxed Herbie down to a lower West Side Manhattan club called the Roxy, where DJs such as Afrika Bambaataa and DST held forth. Had he had a similar process of indoctrination this time?

"Well, there's a tune on the new disc, *Hornets*, which goes back to my *Sextant* album from 1972, that kind of relates to this process. When Bill first proposed this project, he said to me, 'Are you aware there's a whole new subculture that's grown up out of the hip hop arena that uses electronic ambient sounds, drum 'n' bass, and a whole load of other techniques?' I told him I really knew nothing about it, but I was even more amazed when he said that I was one of the key players who had influenced this new movement, and that some of the major discs that had been sampled into this new direction were my recordings *Sextant* and *Dedication* from the early seventies, including my tune *Nobu*, which is on the second of those. Bill went on to say he thought it might be a really good idea for me to put my take on where this music has got to, thus far. So that's basically what we did, and *Future 2 Future*, as its title suggests, is my reaction to this new music of the future, music in which, unbeknownst to me, I had played a hand in developing."

So, I wondered, was that what lay behind the eclectic selection of musicians on the disc, from Rob Swift, Carl Craig, and DXT, to old colleagues such as Wayne Shorter and Jack DeJohnette? "Basically, we took the direction that has been established by the younger players and interpreted it with older, more seasoned musicians, but we put those alongside some others who've really had very little experience. But we also thought we'd bridge the generations by adding players like Charnett Moffett and Chaka Khan. The intention was to put a new kind of twist on a new twist."

So had it been easy for Herbie to immerse himself in the music of this new subculture, and to find a direction for his "reaction" to it?

"To tell you the truth, eventually I went out and listened to a whole lot of it because at the end of the third day of recording I was tired of being in a dither about what was happening. The very first day in the studio, Bill played something to me and said, 'Just react. We'll put it down. Don't think too hard about it.' So I said okay, went and played, then we did another take, and Bill said, 'Great, that was almost perfect.' After three days of this, I really didn't know what was going on, and I was wondering to myself if I was making a mistake trying to do this. So I voiced my concerns to my manager David Passick and to our other partner in this new recording venture, Chuck Mitchell, who had been the president of Polygram's jazz division. Chuck sent over a bunch of discs for me to listen to by Nils Petter Molvaer and some other musicians. And back at home in LA, I talked to my keyboard-playing colleague Darryl Diaz, and he brought me *Roots* and a bunch of other things, and suddenly it clicked, and I said to myself, 'Oh *I see!*' I saw I was in the ballpark, and what the relationship was with *Sextant* and *Nobu*, which I didn't really remember, but I had got out and played a few times. And from that moment, I had a sense of what the whole arena was all about, and I could see it more in perspective. At that stage we still hadn't finished recording the album, but I went back into it knowing that although I didn't know the area too well, I didn't know what not to do, and I could rely more on my own judgement."

It turned out it was a relatively late decision to bring in Wayne Shorter as one of the guest musicians on the disc, but for me, at any rate, he is the album's main catalyst – whatever his knowledge of or familiarity with the context, he transforms the music around him, a view with which Herbie wholeheartedly agrees. "Once he started to play, we kept throwing stuff at him, and the way he plays on the track called *Tony Williams* is just unbelievable. There's another track called *Be Still*, and he altered my whole perception of the piece. It was almost not good enough for his playing, and after he'd played his solo there were a lot of things I wanted to take off and change, to do again, to raise our game to his level. When Wayne arrived he had said he didn't want to know too much in advance about what we were doing. He just put the phones on, started playing, and blew us all away. Bill and I were behind the glass just laughing, what he played was so great. Wayne never wanted to hear anything back, but he did three takes on several pieces, and we liked what he'd done so much we used just about all of it, from all the takes."

The way the Tony Williams track came about is unusual, and will be perhaps the most talked-about element of the new album in jazz circles, as it features a drum track laid down by Williams before he died.

Laswell had been working on a possible album with Williams, and had added basslines to the drums, but that was as far as the project had got. "Everything else on the piece was done as an overdub," said Herbie. "It sounds as if we were playing together as a band in the studio, it's that tight, but for each of us there was never anyone else in the studio when we were recording our respective parts. Bill suggested I do two or three different takes, and since I wasn't hemmed in by any particular harmonic structure I used a different chordal approach on each one, so I was a bit surprised when Bill ended up using two of them together, which sounds a little bit quirky."

The only friction in creating the project came, it seems, when Laswell followed Teo Macero's example and disappeared with the tapes to edit the final album. "He ended up not letting me know when or where he was mixing," recalled Herbie, the pain that this must have caused for such a technological obsessive creeping into his voice. "It did cause a few problems between us afterwards, but I think that now Bill knows I don't like working that way, and I had to fix a few things." In the event he was able to do so relatively easily because Herbie is a partner in the new record company that will issue the disc. Transparent Records was set up between Herbie, David Passick and Chuck Mitchell, and it aims to pick up where his earlier venture, Hancock Records, left off. Verve will still handle Herbie's jazz output, but his crossover ventures, his experimental music and his larger-scale ideas are likely to happen on Transparent.

For a moment, we left the land of technology and the world of music, and think lifestyle. "You know the way *Rolling Stone* magazine stopped just being a music paper and became the pattern for a whole approach to life?" asked Herbie. "Well, that's what I want to happen with Transparent. I want it to be a genreless label – at least that's to say a label that's not limited by genre. And I want it to have sufficient flexibility for new ways of doing things." His grin crept back as he returned to his favourite topic: "I have this desire to explore new avenues of promotion and interactivity. Wouldn't it be great if we could start using the Internet for competitions to remix material we put out on the label?"

12 andrew hill

The highly individual and distinctive playing of Andrew Hill is something I have long admired, since his heyday on the Blue Note label in the 1960s, with albums that appeared as I was beginning my interest in jazz. Subsequently, I have presented his trio on BBC Radio 3, interviewed him for a documentary on Blue Note, and talked to him further on numerous occasions. Most important of all, I've managed to hear his playing whenever possible, including his duo with Archie Shepp, his recent sextet, and the experimental big band with which he toured the UK in 2003. What follows was a feature for *Jazzwise* in June 2000, supplemented by parts of an interview for *The Times* from May 2003.

If you've kept an eye on concert listings, then you'll have seen Andrew Hill's name cropping up quite a bit over the last few years. In Britain alone, there was a Contemporary Music Network tour with three other solo pianists in the early 1990s, then a trio concert at the Queen Elizabeth Hall in 1997, and most recently a duo with Archie Shepp at the same venue in April 2000. And on the other side of the pond, he and Bobby Hutcherson were featured the same month at the Lincoln Center's new "Duets on the Hudson" series at the prestigious Kaplan Penthouse above New York's Juilliard School of Music.

But while concert-goers may have heard quite a bit of Mr Hill in such settings as these, there's been a total silence from him on the recording front, since the last of his projects for the revitalized Blue Note label in 1990, a disc which carried the increasingly ironic title of *But Not Farewell*. However, this year [2001], first with a major guest role on Greg Osby's *Invisible Hand* album, and now his own sextet disc *Dusk*, Andrew Hill is back.

One reason for his absence from the studios is a determination to look forward in everything that he plays. He's always gentlemanly and diplomatic about other musicians, but when we met, I sensed a disappointment in him that so many of his contemporaries are revisiting past glories. He affectionately referred to one or two of his old colleagues doing the rounds of the international circuit playing the same old stuff as "gorillas." He's even more critical of the younger players who have followed the Wynton Marsalis direction in looking back into the tradition.

"Everybody who loves the music probably loves those artists," he said, rocking gently to and fro, and occasionally pointing his trademark dark glasses directly at me, which made eye contact a little difficult. "In a retrospective situation," he continued, "everyone can play the notes and stuff, but they don't have the magic because they've become so homogeneous that something's lost. In our day, we would play, and then the technique would come to fit whatever we wanted to play. But today they develop the technique first, and then play in a kind of chronological isolation. They haven't had direct contact with the masters, and that's where the magic is missing because although you can get a lot of stuff academically, the real feeling, the feeling that creates the magic has to be taught to you. That's where you learn the stuff that's not written, the tones, the colours, the things you can do, and that's what we got from contact with the masters."

The idea of "magic," the joy of new creation, of new ideas and fresh music is vitally important to Hill. American critic Howard Mandel said of him that you can hear him thinking original thoughts as he plays, and anyone who heard his recent concert with Archie Shepp will have seen that process in action, especially in Hill's solo piece. When I met Greg Osby recently, he told me he can't think of anyone who's as consistently inventive and swift to develop as Hill, in whose band he worked ten years ago.

Perhaps paradoxically, Hill himself puts his perpetual quest for the new down to his own contact with one of the "masters," growing up on Chicago's South Side, where he got to know Earl "Fatha" Hines. "I was a small boy, delivering the *Chicago Defender,* and I was his paper boy. Then down near the old Regal Theatre where all the big bands used to come, was the Hurricane Lounge where Gene Ammons performed. Even when I was a little boy I wanted to get paid for performing, so I used to have me a corner there, where I'd take my accordion, play it and do a tap dance. From my having delivered his newspaper, Earl Hines saw me there, and recognized me. He asked 'Can you play piano?'

"I said 'Yes.'

"So then when I passed by with the papers every morning, I'd leave for school a little early because he'd invite me into his house for breakfast and talk and show me things. It was great because in those days music was more accessible as it wasn't an art form. It was the popular music of the community. In those days the record companies recorded what those communities wanted to hear, but today, when everything is driven by the big corporations, nobody at the record companies is looking at the social conditions of society in the same way and making records for them."

Coupled with his concern at the big business that drives the industry is Hill's own acute self-criticism. I wondered why he had not gone on to make records with the trio he brought to London in 1997, with Reggie Workman and Pheeroan AkLaff because when I talked to him on that visit, he was waxing lyrical about their music. But, it seems, when it came to it he didn't think they were "ready" to record.

And then, quite unexpectedly, Michael Dorf at the Knitting Factory asked Hill to come up with a band for the club's 1998 festival that revisited the instrumentation of Hill's 1964 sextet album *Point Of Departure*. After all his earlier strictures about retrospective projects, Hill was adamant to point out that all the music his new band played was newly written. The only connection to the earlier group was the line-up: trumpet, two reeds, piano, bass and drums.

Certainly, one immediately obvious aspect of the resulting album, *Dusk*, is that several of the pieces are through-composed. They seldom conform to the head-solos-head pattern of so much jazz "composition." Also, Hill has created plenty of contrasts, some places where the rhythm section drops out to leave just the horns, and others where he either works in duo with one instrument, notably altoist Marty Ehrlich, or plays entirely alone, especially on a wistful solo called *Tough Love*. This, he said, was all intentional – to create a disc with a feeling of composition about it, but which left his colleagues free to express themselves. When I suggested I could hear overtones of some of Julius Hemphill's trademarks in the way the reeds are voiced, he said, "That's not my idea, I think that's Marty. His attack, the way he pitches, and the way he plays alongside the other saxophonist Greg Tardy, are all things that go back to his contact with Hemphill, but it wasn't a conscious part of the writing process."

So is this disc just a stepping stone in his relentless quest for the new, or does he see himself sticking with the line-up?

"This time," he said, cautiously, "I think I'm in it for the long haul. I can see this band still working and still playing new material a couple of years from now. I've been writing a lot for it for the past two years, and there's stuff we still haven't played yet."

One striking composition on the present disc is called *T.C.* dedicated to the late Thomas Chapin. "Yeah, I met him in my doctor's office. At the time I was suffering from a potentially life-threatening condition and so was he, but unfortunately he didn't make it. So this is in memory of him. I didn't know his work before I met him, but he sent me a bunch of CDs, and I really liked his playing. I encouraged him even when he was very ill to go back to playing, and I heard that he successfully did that before he died."

Hill also sees further recording possibilities for the group, especially since his move from Blue Note to the independent Palmetto label, where he has forged a creative partnership with producer Matt Balitsaris.

So what about other projects?

Hill recently gave up his teaching post, and is now focusing on playing and composing, so we can expect to hear more of him than we have in the last few years. He rather thinks that there won't be too many more one-off appearances like his recent South Bank concert, but he was genuinely elated about his Duets on the Hudson event with Bobby Hutcherson. "We go back a long way, but we were both determined not to get into that retrospective thing. So I wrote some new material, and then we arranged to spend three days together, just playing and working out some of the new music. In fact we didn't need all that time because everything just clicked very fast, and we found new ways of expressing music together. To some of the players on that series it may have been just another gig, but we wanted to make an impact. So we both went out and spent some money on new tuxedos. I hope if everything goes right, we'll do some more duo concerts, and have the chance to wear them again soon."

> Three years on, and Hill was back in Britain for a Contemporary Music Network tour with an Anglo-American big band. His sextet of 2000 had boiled down to a quintet, but it had stayed the course, and proved his perception that this had been a long-term project. His methods and philosophy for the big band were typically novel, and although not all the concerts worked, there was a *frisson* of excitement about everything the band played.

"I've got used to being the best-kept secret in the jazz world," said Andrew Hill, the controversial jazz pianist who brought his big band to Britain this week [May 2003] for a short tour. Most musicians faced with integrating ten strangers into their regular line-up would arrive with a stack of tightly written arrangements, and expect to rehearse hard before playing them roughly the same way every night. But not Hill – his approach is characteristically different.

"Jazz is first and foremost an improvised music," he said. "So I've always had the contention that a big band should be an improvising situ-

Andrew Hill at the Queen Elizabeth Hall, London, 1997 (Derek Drescher)

ation as well. Just think about the way any musician who's spent any period of a time in a large jazz orchestra tells you how boring it is, playing the same parts night after night, so that the only challenge is to see if you can still play it when you're drunk. I've written music where the sections of each piece change from one performance to the next, so that it's not in the least predictable how the programme will develop. Put that in front of a band, and immediately they become sober, sharpen up their act, and begin participating. Their enthusiasm is transmitted to the audience."

How did he feel about having the cream of young British Caribbean players among the personnel, players such as Denys Baptiste, Jason Yarde and Byron Wallen, each of whom is an innovator in his own right? He paused, had another of his characteristic rocks to and fro, and then said slowly, "To me these players have the same intensity and creativity that my groups had in the sixties, but their beat has changed. What they hear in their heads fits the pattern of the day."

One surprising thing about Hill is that he, too, seems to be attuned to the pattern of the day. Unlike many of his contemporaries from the Blue Note stable of 1960s' hard bop players, he has never been content to play in the style of forty years ago. "In bebop, you can go away and not practise for a month," he pointed out, "and then come back and play a magnificent performance. Everything's familiar, you know how to make it a success. But I can't do that. I always want to come up with something different."

He does this successfully by taking time out from performing to write and think. Recently, he won the Danish Jazzpar prize, so for the six months leading up to the April 2003 award ceremony he was writing the music for the Copenhagen presentation, some of which will be played on his British tour. Like many of his compositions, not all of this is straightforwardly accessible, but when I challenged him on the difficulty of his work, he was quick to defend himself with a historical argument.

"Look," he said, "when I started in the '60s, what I was doing was just as experimental, but people didn't perceive it that way. Jazz was still a popular music. It hadn't turned itself into an art form. Listeners had more developed ears, so they could hear what I was doing as part of a continuum. Nowadays, some people find my music from that era rather weird, but it was natural to us and to our audiences. So today, I'm still taking hold of the melodies in my head, and I'm still mainly writing for myself. But my main goal is to make everything I do really musical, so that people who really love music can enter into it and share the experience."

13 abdullah ibrahim

As a schoolboy I collected discs by Dollar Brand, as he was then known. As a concert reviewer, I have subsequently had the privilege of experiencing his playing in many contexts, and this piece, for the May 2002 *Piano* magazine, was written after we met for the first time, when he was my guest on the BBC World Service show *Jazzmatazz*.

On stage, Abdullah Ibrahim cuts an impressive figure: tall, dressed in black, and sitting very upright at the piano, directing his musicians with a nod or a turn of the head. In person, face to face, he's even more impressive, with a firm, powerful handshake and a sense of calm and self-containment that he attributes to years of studying martial arts. He is South Africa's leading jazz pianist, and, particularly since the end of apartheid, one of the most influential musicians on the new generation of players that are emerging in his country.

He was born and brought up in Cape Town, and as a young man he worked in the notorious District Six, the large multicultural area of compact houses, shops, clubs and cinemas that was ethnically cleansed and bulldozed by the apartheid regime. Much of the South Africa he knew and loved as he was growing up has also vanished, but since the late 1960s he has captured the atmosphere of his homeland in music. To do so, he turned his back on a promising career in American cutting-edge jazz with drummer Elvin Jones, in whose band he had been playing from 1966.

"It was time for me to return to my roots, to who I was," he told me, about the period from 1968 to 1974, at the end of which he recorded his extraordinary hit record *Mannenburg*, which features saxophonist Basil Coetzee in a very long extended solo. "That was an extraordinary session," he recalled. "Basil began playing this solo, and it just sounded right. It was one of those moments in jazz when an improvised solo becomes something bigger, almost like a composition, and of course, now it is actually studied in its own right. But it captured a mood of the time, and even the name of the piece had all sorts of resonances for our audience."

Abdullah Ibrahim, 1997 (Peter Symes)

It became so popular that Ibrahim was even coerced into playing it by gangsters who turned up for one of his concerts, and for years he could seldom appear anywhere in South Africa without playing the tune. He was one of the jazz exiles, as they became known, who was brave enough to return to South Africa during the years of struggle. But the impact of the regime, and the after-effects of the Sharpeville killings, had a devastating effect on his career.

As the 1960s began, he had been a member of a pioneering band called The Jazz Epistles, which also included trumpeter Hugh Masekela and saxophonist Kippie Moeketsie. They'd just cut their first album and were about to embark on a national tour, when new laws came in, in the wake of Sharpeville, which effectively forbade their audiences from assembling. The band broke up, and Moeketsie, the inspiration for much of the band's work, and its mentor, chose to remain in South Africa, while Masekela went to New York by way of London, and Ibrahim set off for Switzerland with his wife to be, the singer Sathima Bea Benjamin.

And there fate took a hand in his career.

"We saw in the papers that Duke Ellington was going to be playing a concert in Zurich, where we had settled," recalled Ibrahim. "I couldn't go, as I had to play at my usual nightclub gig with my trio, but Sathima agreed to go, so she could come and tell us all about the concert. Imagine my surprise when I looked up towards the end of the evening and there was Sathima coming into our club with Duke Ellington himself. He liked our music, and within a very few days he had arranged for us to go and make a record in Paris. Sathima sang some tracks with me and the trio, and some on which either Duke or Billy Strayhorn played piano. They didn't know all her tunes, and I remember teaching Billy Strayhorn the chords to *A Nightingale Sang In Berkeley Square*. Before long he'd got the hang of it, and began to prepare to record. As he did the run through of this ballad about a nightingale, he started playing some pretty adventurous ideas. Duke wandered over to the piano and said to him: 'What kind of birds are those, Sweet Pea?' And Strayhorn looked up at him and said, 'I'm playing condors, man.'"

The resulting album, *A Morning In Paris*, was only reissued for the first time on CD quite recently, with several additional tracks that had never been released before, but it marked Ibrahim's first steps onto the world stage. At Ellington's insistence, he followed up the Paris sessions by travelling to the United States, and during his initial visit there, under his original name of Dollar Brand, he made a triumphant debut at the Newport Jazz Festival.

Of all Ibrahim's recent visits to Britain, I have most enjoyed his work with his septet, Ekaya (which means "home"). For this group, as with many of his others, he prefers to dictate his compositions to his musicians, so they learn the pieces by ear, and are not bound to sheet music as they perform. His numbers all evoke a sense of Africa, from the rhythms of the Cape to the melodies drawn from the rich South African choral tradition. But there is always one moment in each concert that I wait for, which is when the other musicians leave the stage, and Ibrahim plays an extended piano solo. He tends to start quietly and then gradually build up the momentum and the excitement, often shuffling his feet along with his playing. When I asked him about that, he smiled his slow smile. "Oh well, that goes back to my first love as a pianist. When I started playing, I listened to all the boogie-woogie records I could find, by players like Albert Ammons and Jimmy Yancey. That was what I grew up on, and that was what I started out playing for local dances, and so it's just become an integral part of my own music!"

14 keith jarrett

I was in the United States making a BBC documentary series about the fiftieth anniversary of Gerry Mulligan's piano-less quartet, when the opportunity came up to visit Keith Jarrett for a lengthy interview. The reason was the imminent release of the double album *Always Let Me Go* by his Standards Trio, but we ended up in a much more wide-ranging discussion, of which the main parts were distilled into this article for the November 2002 issue of *Piano*.

It didn't take more than a few minutes of conversation to realize that Keith Jarrett is not a man to dwell on his past achievements as an unparalleled jazz improviser, a successful bandleader and a distinctive classical soloist. For much of his life, the sheer pace of his creativity and the bewildering scope of his work has kept him firmly focused on either the present or the immediate future and, as an improviser, it is the next concert, the forthcoming encounter with the keyboard, that holds most excitement and fascination for him. However, in the recent past, two events have rather changed his perspective, and given him the opportunity to consider his earlier work.

First, in 1996, he was diagnosed as suffering from ME, or chronic fatigue syndrome. For almost eighteen months he didn't touch a piano, and there then followed a long, slow process of beginning to play again.

Second, earlier this year, his record label ECM invited him to make a selection of his back catalogue to issue in its new :Rarum series.

When I met Jarrett recently, he told me how this had given him the opportunity to take the time to listen again to his earlier work, and, in the case of his recovery from illness, to use the time to re-evaluate his whole approach to the piano.

"When I got sick, I listened to all my old stuff," he recalled. "I had so much time on my hands, I didn't know if I'd ever play again. Half of it struck me as ridiculously poor. I didn't like my long introductions, nor did I like a lot of things about my touch. The sickness gave me the chance to think hard about what I actually heard, and then apply it to what I was able to do in the future. During my illness, I became so weak that I had to figure out a lot of things all over again. When I started to play once more, I hadn't touched the piano for over a year – almost a year and a half in fact – and in many ways I was lucky to have the opportunity to start over again because I discovered new ways of playing that I might otherwise not have investigated. I had to think to myself, what is my touch now?

"One thing I picked up from listening to my recordings was that sometimes I sounded like a horn – a saxophone or a trumpet. I'd always been on the piano's case for not having a voice that sang in that way, capable

Keith Jarrett, 2002 (ECM)

of sustaining a sound as a wind instrument does, and I used my time to reconnect to that horn idea. It's been fundamental to some of my other work, too. When I had the trio in the 1970s with Charlie Haden and Paul Motian, although I think three is a magic number for playing improvised music, I added Dewey Redman on saxophone because, as a composer, many of the things I wanted to write had no outlet until I had a horn to play them. They just weren't possible on the piano alone.

"So I've been investigating areas where I can use the piano to capture some of that horn quality. Partly it's to do with timing. I remember, for example, when I was in his band, how Miles Davis used to come in so perfectly on the beat that even drummers were envious. It's also to do with what you play and what you imply. Charlie Parker used to hint at whole flurries of notes, but not actually play all of them, nor did he produce what notes he did play equally loudly, and for me that's the essence of jazz, to leave a veil over part of what you do so that some aspects remain hidden, and not to put everything out front in the way a player like, for example, Oscar Peterson might.

"In my current group, the Standards Trio, with Jack DeJohnette on drums and Gary Peacock on bass, we're coming up to our twentieth anniversary, but only this summer, during our 2002 European tour, Gary asked me, 'Do you realize how you're sounding? Are you aware of the way you're playing?'

"I said, 'Yeah.'

"He told me, 'Well, I don't know what to say, but whatever it is, keep doing it!'

"In fact I'm not only aware of this singing quality in my playing, but I can't help it. At the same time, I hope I never actually reach the point where I hear the same thing I want to achieve actually coming out of the piano. Part of my approach to playing is to want my personality to shift from me to the music."

At this point in our conversation, we get sidetracked into a discussion about personality. Jarrett has often gone on record as saying that he likes to try and empty his mind completely before one of his long solo concerts, so that he relies on no preconceived formulae to create his vast improvisations. He told me that sometimes, as a consequence, he feels elements of the personality of the audience creeping into his playing. In a graphic illustration of this, he was talking to the concert organizer after his first solo recital in Rio de Janiero, who congratulated him on fitting in a particularly obscure local dance rhythm into his playing. Jarrett was astonished because he had never consciously listened to that dance form before, and was completely unaware it had crept into his improvisation.

"It must come from their sensibilities because my mind's empty, and I get the message of playing their music. It's happened to me half a dozen times in half a dozen countries."

In respect of ensemble playing, he sees the work of his current Standards trio as an exercise in suppressing their individual personalities in favour of the music of the group as a whole. It is a process that has become more and more apparent in the trio's last three albums, starting with their creative reinterpretations of well-known songs on *Whisper Not*, moving on to their first collective exploration of free playing on *Inside Out*, and culminating in the new double CD *Always Let Me Go*, which takes free playing to a new level of co-operative integration.

It might seem a paradox that a band that made its reputation performing the standard repertoire in a fresh and exciting way should now opt to play with no preconceived structure and form, but Jarrett, who suggested the idea two years ago to his colleagues during a long transatlantic flight, and then tried it out in the first hall they came to where the acoustics seemed suitable, sees it as part of a continuous process.

"The key word in our development is personality. At best, we erase our personalities, and each of us becomes, in a non-derogatory sense, a pawn in the process of creating music. We let our hands do what they seem to want to do, and we try as little as possible to have that part of our brains called personality be involved. When it creeps in, and I hear it happening in my own playing, it's an irritant, not a good thing. Gary talks about Zen at this point, about involving less of yourself, and entering the spirit of the flow of sound."

Certainly, the new album is a remarkable example of creative empathy, the group setting up atmospheres, dismantling them, moving into passages of hard-swinging four-to-the-bar time, and then equally rapidly dissolving into a new mood, with the balance between piano, bass and drums shifting all the time. Throughout, there are Jarrett's usual qualities of grace, lyricism and sensitivity.

To make the point forcibly about suppressing individual personalities in favour of the group sound, he talked next not about his new album, but about *Whisper Not*, the concert recorded in the Palais de Congrès in Paris at the end of his 1999 comeback tour from illness.

"We recorded several performances on that tour, and we'd played what we all thought was a marvellous evening in Verona. It was a beautiful recording, done outdoors in front of 12,000 people who were so silent and attentive it was as if they had disappeared and reappeared at the end. By contrast, none of us was happy at the time with the Paris set. I had been dealing with a bull of a piano, with such a stiff action that for it to sound fluid at all was a miracle. We all hated the sound in the hall, and Gary, in particular, disliked the way his bass felt in the room. So if all we had to go on was our imaginations, we would have issued the Verona concert and never even listened to Paris at all. But when I got home I did listen to it, and was amazed by what I heard. Maybe it was because it was the last concert of the tour, and I was playing with masses of energy because I wasn't worried about having a relapse that would have prevented me from playing the next night, or maybe it was because we already had the Verona concert in the can, but we played incredibly as a group. So much so I called Gary over to listen to the tapes. I particularly wanted him to listen to a couple of his solos. He said, 'I didn't play any good solos that night.' But he did, except that they didn't sound like any Gary Peacock solo I'd heard before, and by losing himself, his own personality, the music had gained. It's a great example of how even those that make the music don't always know how it sounds because so many elements go into it."

Jarrett believes that one of the things that has allowed this trio to develop to the point where it can abandon the standard repertoire and continue to make fresh and absorbing music by playing with no preconceived ideas is the level of trust that has built up over twenty years. "If you're playing songs, and the other guys know them, you don't need the four-dimensional level of trust that free playing involves; you only need a couple of dimensions. They start playing the song, they fall into time, and I can play a solo on top of that. But with free playing, there's always the idea that the others understand what you understand. You'll never know that for sure, of course, but you can often hear in their playing that there are parallel universes at work. When Jack finds a place to play that is not exactly where Gary is, but relates to it, then that allows me the freedom to choose one of their approaches, or to come up with a third thing. I might play the hint of a tempo and Jack immediately comes up with the suggestion of other things that we can follow or not as we choose."

There seemed to me to be a parallel here with Jarrett's much-celebrated solo concerts, which he approaches with an extraordinary mixture of rigour and self-criticism, in order to achieve the same kind of freshness he finds with the trio. "I have two challenges in solo concerts," he said, "to come up with good music, and not to come up with good music I've come up with before, and the second is the greater of those challenges. But there are personal challenges too because when you are backstage before you go on to improvise, you really know nothing about what's going to happen. That fact alone is a magnet, drawing you to be curious, and you think to yourself, 'I know I've done this before, but I really know nothing about the process.' That is certainly something that is common ground with the trio, where I'm now concerned more about opening a door on the process of improvising than presenting an object."

This is in contrast to the fastidious way Jarrett presented his interpretations in the classical side of his career – something he re-evaluated after suffering a nervous breakdown in 1985. Since that time he has continued to perform works by Mozart and Bach, both composers he identifies with as having been improvisers, but he no longer plays the range of material or keeps up the kind of schedule he did in the early 1980s. His recent illness focused his mind about both his attitude to playing classical music, and to composing, which he now sees as too slow and time-consuming a pursuit.

"Since I was ill, I now feel committed to playing because I now know how fragile life can be. Any composer can go on editing their symphony until they die, always saying, 'It's almost ready.' But as a player you have a stark choice, you can play or not play. When I was sick I couldn't play, and that was an amazing wake-up call as to who I am. After performing so many classical recitals, I had come to think that something was missing compared to my improvised work, and I realized it was that I knew every note that was going to be played already. I could play them really well, or not really well, but what difference would that make to my life?

"So the only area of the classical world I've really gone back to often since 1985 is Mozart. To me his music is one of the few examples in classical music where the piano is really supposed to be singing. If it doesn't sing, it sounds horrible. It looks so simple on paper that when you're a kid you hate it, but around ten years ago or so I thought I'd become the right age to play Mozart, and I recorded two albums of concerti with the Stuttgart Chamber Orchestra. If I hadn't gotten ill, Dennis Russell Davies and I would already have recorded a third album, which if it eventually goes ahead will include the D Major 'Coronation' concerto – the very first concerto I was ever given to play as a kid."

So what did Jarrett see as his contribution to the performance of the classical repertoire?

"Most interpreters have read their history, and they know their ornaments, and they've read up on Mozartian technique or Beethoven's dynamics. But they don't know what it's like to improvise or compose, and in that respect I think I have an inroad into Mozart that most other interpreters might not have. I think many of those who perform the classical piano repertoire are divorced from what those composers were actually doing. It's a conundrum because if Mozart was alive I'm not so sure he'd want to hear his old pieces all that badly, he'd be writing new ones; but I wonder if what he did hear would please him, with on the one hand plenty of performances sounding largely the same from a number of different players, and on the other, several that sound radically different, with people taking too many liberties."

So where did Jarrett himself stand on liberties? Would he, for example, improvise his own cadenzas, as his fellow Miles Davis alumnus Chick Corea did at his Festival Hall performance of Mozart's Concerto No. 20 a couple of years ago?

"No, I use the ones Mozart thoughtfully supplied at every chance I get. As a composer, despite the fact I'm also an improviser, it might surprise you to realize that I don't expect liberties to be taken with my music. As a conductor, I'd take much of it so steadily it might even be boring, but that's the way I hear it. So my contribution with Mozart's music is to play it very faithfully, as though I was reading the notes he put down."

Mention of his Mozart recordings brings us back again to his consideration of his past work, and his recently-issued retrospective :Rarum collection on ECM. There are no examples of his classical playing there because Jarrett, in his usual conscientious and thoughtful way, has interpeted the idea of "collected works" to mean his own compositions, so the double CD is entirely filled with his original pieces.

"One thing that guided me was to include things that I wish more people had heard. So there are a couple of pieces there that only ever appeared fleetingly on LP, and have never made it to CD up until this point. The other things I wish were better known are my recordings on pipe organ and on clavichord. I first played the organ when I was spending some time in France in the 1960s, and I was introduced to a nearby church with an old pipe organ. I was immediately lost in its world of sound. I loved the possibilities in this mechanical instrument, the actual sound of the air going through the pipes, and the changes in pitch that happen if a stop isn't pulled fully out. So my explorations on that instrument take a direction that I think very few improvisers have followed, and where I think there's plenty of room for more to be done.

"The clavichord is a similar kind of exploration. I think I'm a master of meeting a new instrument and finding out what it can do because of improvising all my life. Of course I wasn't a complete stranger to the clavichord, and I had some idea of what it could do. The fascination with it is that the pitch changes constantly because of the pressure you exert on the string. This led me towards making contrapuntal linear statements with very few voices because in some ways the instrument itself demands that kind of playing. If I succeeded in making something original, it's because I let the instrument lead me, just the same way that I always have on my solo concerts with piano. I've been playing pianos all my life, they're all so different from one another, and vary so much, that you sometimes think you're playing another type of instrument entirely!"

15 brian kellock

A double winner at the BBC Jazz Awards, with prizes in both 2002 and 2003, Brian Kellock has put himself on the map as one of the UK's leading pianists. Because he chooses to remain based in Scotland, he has not always been recognized by the London-based critical fraternity as the creative force he is, whether on disc, on air, or on the bandstand. This interview with Brian (and Caber Records' Tom Bancroft) is expanded from an article published in *Piano* in September 2001.

The most lively and innovative place in the British jazz scene at present is Edinburgh. For the last few years, the city has become home to a generation of musicians who have pushed at the boundaries of jazz, including a lively cross-fertilization with the flourishing Scottish traditional music scene. For example, bands such as drummer John Rae's Celtic Feet combine the sounds of jazz piano and saxophone with the traditional fiddle playing of Eilidh Shaw and the concertina of Simon Thoumire. Equally, saxophonist Tommy Smith's projects have included musical interpretations of the work of the Scottish poet Edwin Morgan, such as *Beasts Of Scotland*, and Tommy has also been the guiding light behind the Scottish National Jazz Orchestra, which is now one of Britain's leading big bands.

All this activity has been faithfully documented by several independent record companies, ranging in size from Glasgow's medium-sized Linn label, down to Tommy Smith's fledgling Spartacus imprint. Most imaginative and unconventional of all, however, is the Caber label, established by drummer, bandleader, composer and former medical practitioner Tom Bancroft. And as well as providing a platform for Bancroft's own playing in his trio AAB (a band which produced one of the highlights of the 2000 Bath International Music Festival and has gone on to be a popular fixture on the UK circuit), Caber Music is home to one of Britain's finest jazz pianists, Edinburgh-born Brian Kellock.

Brian has never followed his fellow Scots pianists Dave Newton, Paul Harrison and Steve Hamilton to a career south of the border. He has remained firmly based in Edinburgh, where he read music at university during the 1980s, going on to become one of the city's main jazz pianists.

"I like it here," he said, as we met in a pub not far from the Royal Mile. "I've always liked it here, and I've not been of the turn of mind that's felt it's important to go to London to prove yourself. You can do it here, and if you start making contacts in Europe and elsewhere in the world, it's as easy to fly to those places from Scotland as anywhere else. So I prefer to stay here in Scotland, which offers a nice way of life. Having said that, I do find that to make a living in jazz here, I've had to diversify quite a lot. It keeps my interest going, of course, to play in a number of different contexts, but it does mean that I've never entirely settled on one style. If I were asked to give up all the other stuff in order to concentrate on one thing – I'm not sure I could actually do it."

Indeed, the range of Brian's work is quite remarkable. He not only works frequently with Celtic Feet and the Scottish National Jazz Orchestra, but he is the accompanist of choice for a huge number of musicians, from singer Carol Kidd to Australian trumpeter and multi-instrumentalist James Morrison, with whom he has toured throughout Europe and Oceania since 1995. The pitfall of being such a popular accompanist is

Brian Kellock and friends (Brian Kellock)

that as the 1990s went on, Brian had less time available to develop an independent career, but slowly, surely and with considerable flair, that is what he has most recently been doing, mainly with his own trio which includes John Rae on drums and bassist Kenny Ellis.

The trio's first album for Caber, made in 1998, was *Something's Got To Give: Portraits Of Fred Astaire*.

"I've always loved standards," Brian pointed out, "and I've tried to learn as many tunes as possible during my career. I think that goes back to one of my earliest gigs at the Edinburgh Jazz Festival, supporting the altoist Peter King. On the first gig he asked me if I knew *Speak Low*, and at the time I didn't. A couple of days later, when I was backing him again, he asked me again if I knew it, and I cursed myself for not having taken the trouble to learn it in between. So ever since then, I've really immersed myself in standards, so that I know a great number of them. The songs that Fred Astaire sang or danced to are nearly all fantastic, so for this trio disc I wanted to draw a collection of them together. In doing so, I wanted to model our approach on the playing of some of the great trios of the 1950s, like, for example, the one led by Wynton Kelly. His kind of playing tends to be quite compact – it's not about massive, long solos – and I prefer that kind of focus to the huge sprawling landscapes of some later types of trio."

From around 1996, Brian's own trio has played regularly at Henry's Cellar Bar in Edinburgh, an atmospheric basement club that is very much a key part of the city's burgeoning jazz scene, and in the summer of 2001 the trio released its best album to date, *Live At Henry's*. According to Tom Bancroft, the club is very much Brian's natural habitat, and Tom approached producing the album rather as a wildlife documentary-maker might have tackled a film about a rare and wonderful beast on home turf.

"The Edinburgh scene is actually quite small, in the sense that there is a limited number of live venues," says Bancroft. "So it's a bit like living in a tiny house. You get fed up with the size of the bathroom or the kitchen, but then when you go away for any length of time you long to be home. Also, Henry's club has had a very diverse musical policy, and when it was originally started by a Chinese guy called Kulu, he set it up to have drum 'n' bass one night, hip hop the next, and straightahead jazz the one after. Brian's played there right through all that, and he's still there now, although the club's now got a more jazz-orientated policy under its new director Kirsten Douglas, who's helped bring in a better piano, a PA system and so on. All those years of appearing there mean that Brian's worked hard at playing to an audience that has a very wide range of musical expectation, and he's built up a real rapport with them.

Mind you, Henry's is such a small, intimate club, it's a bit like the Village Vanguard in New York, where you've got complete contact with the audience. There's no sense of distance between the listener and the performer, and we've tried to capture that on the disc, right down to Brian's squeaky chair which we couldn't equalize out of the mix."

If you were to listen to the disc as a blindfold test, the first thing that stands out about it is that it might be the product of a live recording by a top-flight American band because the trio has the same kind of confident, aggressive, all-out attack as many American groups, an ingredient that is often missing, or toned-down, in many a European ensemble. But it also has the kind of delicate dynamic control one might find in the playing of, say, Ahmad Jamal, especially on a version of George Shearing's *Conception* that draws the live audience and the album listener into the performance through the skilful use of restraint and quiet, amid some more dramatic moments.

Elsewhere on the disc, further such dramatic moments reveal just what an inventive and skilled improviser Brian is. A version of Lennie Tristano's challenging piece *Lennie's Pennies* has Kellock apparently squeezing an impossible number of notes into each bar, as the trio takes off in support of his imaginative inventions. Although, as he says, Brian has played most styles of jazz, his real forte is this kind of hard-bop playing, and he is at his most impressive on pieces such as Hank Jones's *Chant* (a piece he describes as "a great catchy wee tune from a great, classy pianist"), or Dizzy Gillespie's *Sho' Nuff*, which has echoes of Bud Powell in its phrasing and shape. However, in his version of the piece, Brian displays one of his specialities, which is to play incredibly rapid bebop lines in unison between his two hands, something not even Powell himself liked to do all that often.

From my own experiences of hearing Brian at the club, it would be hard to disagree with Tom Bancroft, who said that in this setting you catch, "each line fresh, with a tang of surprise, constantly seeking the new twist over the harmony, pushing himself to get across all he has to say." But solely to focus on this aspect of Brian's work would be to miss the point he made earlier about his deliberate policy of diversity. For example, when we met, he'd also recently issued a duo disc with the singer Tam White, but the local record store had plenty of other examples of his work, notably as an accompanist to singers Fionna Duncan and Carol Kidd.

"I've always liked playing for singers, ever since I was doing classical things in university," he said. "To work with Carol, Fionna or Tam takes me across a range of different styles, even if each of them is actually singing the same song. It's nice to hear their different interpretations, and change my approach accordingly. I'd worked with Tam on and off for years, going back to the days of Tam White and the Dexters in the late eighties. That was an nine-piece band, with a four-man brass section, leaning towards R&B, and a few of the songs that came into our duo repertoire date back to those days. But a lot more of them are new, including pieces that he'd written specifically for our duo, which began in the late 1990s when we played support for the Average White Band at a gig in Perth. It went down very well, and we decided to do more things together when the chance came up."

Perhaps the most startling aspect of Brian's diversity, however, came in his recent formation of a new Edinburgh-based band to celebrate the legacy of Fats Waller. I had not expected a player whose real forte seemed to be hard bop to have much interest in tackling the stride repertoire of the 1920s and 1930s, but I had underestimated the breadth of Brian's interest.

"Fats was a genius, and larger than life, but I don't think you can listen to any of his music without getting a big smile on your face," he suggested. "I think his music crosses a lot of boundaries, audiences seem to love it, and as my career's gone on, I've done quite a bit of research, listening to his recordings, and also studying the books of his transcriptions. All his music's a joy, I think, although in trying to play almost any of the transcriptions I've got, you soon realize what a formidable pianist Fats was, and I find some of them virtually impossible. That's partly just down to the physical aspects of what he was doing. When he played his stride left hand, he could stretch a thirteenth, which is impossible for me because I've just got tiny wee lady's hands, so I've had to work out other ways round those left-hand figures. He was simply a stunning piano player, and it's not just the left hand because in some of his right-hand configurations, the patterns he played were concert pianist quality!"

16 diana krall

For the cover story of the June 1999 edition of *Jazzwise*, I wrote what turned out to be quite a controversial piece on Diana Krall. It provoked a significant reaction from several quarters, and not least from my good friend, and professional Canadian, Gene Lees, who reprinted it in his *Jazzletter* along with his own spirited defence of the way she was being marketed to the public. The gist of his argument was that she had to "accept the necessity of publicity and the building of a 'Name', but the very process makes you want to run and hide from it." And he also (incorrectly) implied that, in common with the sentiments of many a dyed-in-the-wool jazz fan, I "did not want" her to be popular, and saw her commercial success as anathema because she had "sold out." As it transpires, in her 2004 disc *The Girl In The Other Room* she has, as she suggested to me she would in due course, come to the point where she's ready to write fresh material of her own. The record includes a number of songs co-written with her husband Elvis Costello. Yet, at the same time, she has more than risen to the potential noted by Gene, when he wrote, "we need excellent interpreters of classic song, and Diana is evolving into that." I think that makes it one-all, in terms of journalists' perceptions.

Here is the original piece, as it appeared in *Jazzwise*, marking one significant step on the way in Diana Krall's progress to her current position of international stardom.

You get the impression after talking to her for a while that it's a relief for Diana Krall to focus on her musical career. From what she says, plenty of interviews in Britain and in the United States have concentrated on her appearance, and in particular her clothes – the diaphanous off-the-shoulder dresses from her last *Love Scenes* album – in other words, on her image as a blonde bimbo who can sing and play piano.

Her "take me seriously as a musician" attitude fits with the fact that, in jazz company, she has always seemed able to slough off her cleverly contrived image and communicate directly to knowledgeable and enthusiastic audiences with all the immediacy, swing and instrumental talent that marked her out as exceptional for her mentors Ray Brown and Jimmy Rowles. I've heard her in a club setting, such as Ronnie Scott's or the Iridium, and she inhabits this milieu naturally and without affectation, something she does even more effectively in front of a festival crowd, such as the broadcast sets from Wigan I introduced recently on Radio 3's *Jazz Notes*, which drew some of the most plentiful and appreciative listeners' letters of the last twelve months.

And yet, the packaging of Diana Krall moves on inexorably, and in company with some new and dramatic pictures that have her in formal black against French windows, a grand piano and tasteful oil paintings, or coyly informal in a casual dress and open-toed sandals, her new album *When I Look In Your Eyes* makes a firm bid for what they call "MOR" – the "middle of the road" audience. As well as more cuts by her trio (occasionally augmented to a quartet with either Jeff Hamilton or Lewis Nash on drums) roughly half the disc backs her vocals and small group with a studio orchestra arranged and directed by Johnny Mandel.

Johnny Mandel's no slouch when it comes to providing an orchestral platform for a singer, and his work for Frank Sinatra (such as *Ring A Ding Ding!*) put him in the very highest echelon of arrangers. However, the Johnny Mandel of today is not so much the man who played brass in the Boyd Raeburn and Jimmy Dorsey bands, or arranged for Basie and Artie Shaw. Rather, he's the Grammy-winning composer of *Shadow Of Your Smile* from the *Sandpiper*, and a man who's respected the world over for giving the full orchestral treatment to a ballad. Even so, he has many admirers within the jazz community. "While jazz fans abhor the string section," wrote Gene Lees in his book *Arranging the Score*, "musicians know there is no more subtle and transparent texture against which to set a solo, whether vocal or instrumental." And what Mandel has done is to give Diana Krall an orchestral palette as subtle and transparent in texture as the garments she wears in her soft-focus fashion photos. But is this the right direction for her? And is the pursuit of the crossover hit marginalizing a genuinely attractive jazz talent to its long-term detriment?

You can tell a little of how a musician's career is going from the kind of guest appearances they choose to make, and while the jazz community will have warmed to her recent duo with Fred Hersch on his latest album to raise money for AIDS charities, her appearance as the singer of *Why Should I Care* over the closing credits of the Clint Eastwood film *True Crime* is a more significant clue, and her walk-on parts on albums by the Chieftains and Rosemary Clooney are others. This is not just a jazz singer and pianist, but someone who appears to want to be thought of as a star.

Perhaps the most intriguing thing about this stage in Diana Krall's career, now the focus is shifting to her as a singer with an orchestra, rather than as a small group pianist who sings, is that when she first decided to be a musician she had no thoughts about being a vocalist, and concentrated on piano. This goes back to schooldays when she failed to pass the audition for her local youth choir: "I auditioned for a soprano," she said, "and the choir director, who was a very good and well-meaning man, was trying to push my range. I was straining to make these high notes, and getting so stressed that it was really quite an achievement even to try to audition for the youth choir.

"I didn't pass, and it just devastated me. Nowadays I wish I'd had the confidence to ask to be put in the back with the boys, where I could flirt

Diana Krall in London, 1998 (Peter Symes)

to my heart's desire and sing tenor. I also think now that it's important not to stereotype yourself as a soprano because you're a woman, but back then I really did develop a complex because I thought I couldn't sing high enough. As time's gone on, my voice is getting lower, but to be honest I didn't really feel comfortable singing until I did the album *All For You* which was only three years ago."

Pushed further, she said that developing her voice is a constant process, that she wasn't finally happy until *Love Scenes* was in the can, but that now: "I know what I can do, and I know what I'm shooting for artistically."

Her confidence as a singer began to regain ground for the first time when she left the Vancouver Island area of her native Canada, and became a student at Boston's Berklee College of Music. "My teacher there, Ray Santisi, encouraged me to sing. At first, I'd been the pianist in a vocal jazz ensemble, getting quite frustrated because several of the singers didn't play piano, or didn't know the keys, so I ended up singing in the group as well, but never really in public."

Everything changed when she moved to Los Angeles to study with Jimmy Rowles. There, she said, "it was sinking in that it's not your voice, not whether you have an operatic voice or not, but what you do with it that counts. If you want to sing you should sing. I was still pretty much a kid when I went to study with him, and I'd spend every day at his house and I'm still getting to grips with things he taught me. The beauty of the music for a start. Jimmy Rowles was not flashy, but he was incredibly complex harmonically in his knowledge, which extended from music in general to Debussy and Ravel in particular. The way he played and sang was very, very subtle, and the beauty of the music came through in the way he played and sang songs like *Poor Butterfly*, *Nature Boy* or *How Deep Is The Ocean*. Those things sunk in while I was there, but I'm still processing that, and coming to terms with his whole artistry. But the other thing he taught me was not to take myself too seriously, even though I took the music itself very seriously."

Perhaps it's the very power and depth of Jimmy Rowles as an influence that's made Diana Krall look over her shoulder into the musical past for inspiration, rather than the present. She's a dramatic contrast, for instance, to her one-time school classmate, trumpeter Ingrid Jensen, who has followed a very similar route from the same high-school band to today's New York scene. But whereas Ingrid works on her own compositions, and plays with cutting-edge colleagues such as Dwayne Burno and Bill Stewart, as well as having a musical agenda that is to do with advancing the cause of female instrumentalists in jazz, Diana still plays standards, and mimics the instrumentation and genre of Nat King Cole's trio.

She went quickly on to the defensive when I challenged her on this: "I am a storyteller, and I play the piano, which is the most challenging thing for me at the moment, and always has been. Singing's a challenge too. But as far as compositions go, I feel like I'm studying my Shakespeare, and I'm not ready to write and direct my own play yet. I'm studying songs from Jerome Kern to Joni Mitchell, and there's a lot of music there – it's not an excuse, but I'm not ready to write. And I'm fulfilled by performing standards – I don't see too many people singing songs any more."

So, when the call came from Johnny Mandel, he caught her at something of an artistic crossroads. "I wanted to do more with my trio, and I hadn't really thought about making an album with strings. I wasn't really comfortable with a complete switchover. So, to me, this is the best of both worlds: the Diana Krall trio with Johnny Mandel orchestrating some of the tunes."

Mandel has brought his usual artistry and subtlety to the charts, and his ravishing scoring complete with bass clarinet and flute at the start of *When I Look In Your Eyes* is both a perfect starting point for Diana's regular guitarist Russell Malone, and for her own narrative skill with the lyrics: "The story's all right there, you just have to sing it. But like reading a poem to someone you have to get inside it so that people believe you."

For me, the problem with this is that the songs Diana gets inside best are the quirky, funny, occasionally *double entendre* pieces she does as light and frothy parts of her trio sets. Dave Frishberg's *Peel Me A Grape*, from the *Love Scenes* album is typical, or *Popsicle Toes* from the new album with its risqué storyline: "you load your Pentax when I'm in the nude... I'd like to feel your warm Brazil and touch your Panama." On these, she sings and plays her best, hemmed in neither by the arrangement or any instrumental constraints. On the uptempo jazz numbers with the trio it's the same story, her artful rephrasing of the vocal on *Devil May Care* is mirrored by the offcentre accents of her piano solo, as well as by the intuitively placed stabbing guitar chords from Malone.

But just because these are the songs that Diana makes uniquely her own doesn't mean that they're automatically the most popular. Her straightahead ballads were the favourites of those who wrote in after her recent *Jazz Notes* broadcasts, and she's put in a perfect trio miniature of *I Can't Give You Anything But Love* on the new album. Surrounding it, though, are the Mandel pieces. I find it hard to get worked up about them, in the same way I find the *Mona Lisa* end of Nat Cole's repertoire less compelling than his quicksilver jam session piano or his jaunty jazz vocals with the trio. There's one moment on her new album when Diana's quartet is sailing happily along during *Let's Fall In Love* when they unexpectedly get snagged on the underwater trawl nets of the string section. What's more, the sultry rendition of *I've Got You Under My Skin* sounds more like a parody of a torch singer than the real thing. So there's an unexpected touch of irony in her comment that "there's no question that the strings shine a new light on some of these tunes. I usually have a clear idea of what I want to do, but collaborating with other artists is always a great learning experience. We worked really hard on making sure all the parts fit together correctly. Really, it's a jazz group improvising as usual – the strings are just another instrument."

Maybe, but to me they don't really seem to have made a genuine connection. There's Diana's group improvising as usual, and then there's the orchestra.

In terms of popular success, I'm sure I'm barking up the wrong tree. *When I Look In Your Eyes* has all the hallmarks of an immensely popular album that will be gracing elevators and restaurant sound systems for years to come. I just think it's a shame that the edge and originality of Diana Krall's talent for singing and playing frothy songs in a swinging small group is being pushed aside by a piece of image-making far more threatening than the clothes she wears or the way she's photographed.

17 john lewis

While researching *Groovin' High*, my biography of Dizzy Gillespie, I became intrigued by the significant role of pianist John Lewis in the development of Dizzy's 1946 big band, not least because it was this ensemble that was the midwife for the Modern Jazz Quartet. I had a chance to discuss this with both Ray Brown and Milt Jackson as I was working on *Groovin' High*. Unfortunately, I didn't have the opportunity to talk to John Lewis at that time, but we subsequently made up for it with this conversation for *Piano* magazine, which appeared in the July 2000 issue.

"The thing about John Lewis," said Jacques Loussier, when I talked to him recently, "is that whereas I'm a classical pianist interested in playing jazz, he's a jazz pianist interested in playing the classics." And like so many spur-of-the-moment aphorisms, there's more than a grain of truth in it.

Lewis built his reputation as a modern jazz musician, a bebop pioneer, playing in Dizzy Gillespie's big band, Charlie Parker's quintet, the Miles Davis Nonet, and, most notably, the Modern Jazz Quartet (MJQ), itself an offshoot of Gillespie's rhythm section of the late 1940s. Yet from his schooldays to the present, Lewis has had an abiding interest in the classical tradition, and in performing music that brings this together with jazz. In the 1950s and 60s, he was a prime mover in what his long-term colleague Gunther Schuller named "third stream" territory, between the two traditions.

For much of its forty-year life, that was also a major preoccupation of the MJQ, and if the group will be remembered for one thing, apart from its crusade to get jazz into the concert hall, it will be for the delicate contrapuntal interplay between Lewis's cerebral piano and the bluesy vibraharp of the late Milt Jackson. In Lewis's solo playing, a career that began between 1974 and 1981 when the MJQ was temporarily out of action, and revived after the group finally broke up in 1994 with the death of its drummer Connie Kay, he has always found a place for genuine baroque

John Lewis, 1996 (Derek Drescher)

music alongside his own latterday experiments in counterpoint. The two extremes are to be found in his solo recordings: a 1984 set of his interpretations of Bach's forty-eight preludes and fugues on the one hand, and a bluesy, yet elegant, all-out jazz recital from 1990, issued as *The Private Concert* on the other.

Late last year [1999], Lewis's solo career took another huge leap forward with a new album called *Evolution*, which combines some new material with a reworking of many of his own favourite compositions from the past, including *Two Degrees East, Three Degrees West* and his best-known piece *Django*.

Like most things about Lewis's career, the album title was quite deliberate.

"It's called *Evolution*," he said, "because I think I've evolved over the years, and especially since the time when the quartet was performing so frequently. Lately I've had more time to devote to the piano, and I'm enjoying myself having completely fallen in love with the instrument all over again."

One thing that seems to have got even more refined over the years is his ability to allude to ideas without ever making them completely explicit. I suggested to him that his new version of *Two Degrees East*, for example, hints at the stride style of Fats Waller or Art Tatum in this way, and he agreed: "One of the things I specially like about jazz is that it's not necessary actually to produce a rhythmic beat. You can imply it, so that it appears to be there all the time."

Another surprise was that as an ex-colleague of Dizzy Gillespie and Charlie Parker, who specialized in taking standard popular tunes of the 1940s and creating new melodies over the same chord sequences, I would have expected him to have adopted their reworking of British bandleader Ray Noble's song *Cherokee*, which they retitled *Koko*. But not a bit of it. His version remains remarkably true to Noble's original. "Well," he said, "I think it was a wonderful piece to start with. I enjoyed playing it as it was written, but it is a fantastic piece for virtuoso improvisers, and when I was in Barcelona recently to receive an award, the Spanish band with whom I played used *Cherokee* as their closing piece, and gave everyone a chance to show off their technical prowess. It's still a jam session favourite in its original form."

A more recent composition on the album is his own *For Ellington*, this particular performance having been recorded during the year of the ducal centenary. The tune is, unusually, in waltz time. "When I was writing it," he recalled, "I had in mind the 3/4 of gospel music and also the feeling that Ellington himself captured in his own piece *Come Sunday*. More than that, there's something of Ellington's *Ring Dem Bells* as well. I originally recorded the piece some years back on a MJQ album called *For Ellington*, and on that there was a real chance to ring the bells, using Milt Jackson's vibraharp. On the solo disc I tried to get that same feeling using just the piano."

Atmospheric evocation is a special skill of Lewis's, and his most unusual composition on the new disc is called *At The Horse Show*. He laughed when I asked about it, saying, "I like horses. Show horses, race horses, and also drawings and paintings of horses. For example, I've always liked nineteenth-century lithographs of English racing and hunting. I had a wonderful experience in Vienna when my wife and I were there, seeing the Spanish riding school, and the famous Lipizzaner horses. Well, as you know, they're white horses. But on this occasion the star turn was a black and beautiful horse, which was just incredible, and it was seeing this horse that inspired me to write the piece."

A sense of place is equally important in Lewis's music, and one old composition he has gone back to, and reinterpreted in his recent disc, is called *Afternoon In Paris*. I wondered if this dated from the time when he was writing a whole series of French-inspired pieces for the MJQ with titles like *Vendome*, but it turns out to be even older. "I originally recorded it in the early fifties with Sonny Rollins and J. J. Johnson," he told me. "That was a kind of jam session, with everyone just blowing on the tune, and I've come back many times since to explore the tune in more detail.

"Another older piece I've come back to, with French connections, is my composition *Django*, which I wrote back in the 1950s, not long after his death. He was the first European jazz musician to make an impact on me, and I had first heard his playing in 1944 or 45 during the war, when I was in Rouen, in France. A buddy and I were on a pass, and we'd gone into a small bar. There was a jukebox there, and we put on a recording he'd made as a duo with trumpeter Bill Coleman. I thought it was some of the most incredible playing I had ever heard, and I got to meet him later on, when he came to New York, where he was invited by Duke Ellington. I was playing on 52nd Street with Dizzy at the Famous Door, and Django would come and stay with us all night long. I still miss him – not least because all his life he was a continuously developing musician, always developing, and never stuck in one period or style.

"I think my next visit to Paris was with Dizzy Gillespie in 1948. We had a very rough crossing, and Dizzy and I were the only two members of the band who didn't get extremely seasick. The rest of the band were all just about finished. One good thing about that was that lots of the other passengers were affected as well, so Dizzy and I had our choice of just about anything we wanted to eat from everything on the menu, all to ourselves. To try and take the fellows' minds off the voyage, I did do some teaching on the boat, but the main teacher for all of us in that band was Dizzy. He dictated the notes for many of the pieces we recorded and the way we would play them. I started writing music seriously when I was in his band, beginning with something I'd written even earlier which I turned into *Two Bass Hit* for bassist Ray Brown, who I thought was a player made in heaven because he carried on the great innovations of Jimmy Blanton with Duke Ellington a few years before.

"Of course, a little later than my time with Dizzy, I was involved in writing and arranging for another great trumpeter, Miles Davis, for the *Birth of the Cool* sessions. What I was trying to do there was to find new ways to use the instrumentation of his nonet which included tuba and French horn. Especially the tuba because the musician involved, Bill Barber, was and still is a remarkable player. So I tried to use the possibilities these instruments offered in a polyphonic way, so you'll hear a couple of melodies going on simultaneously with contrasting instrumental colours in my pieces for that group.

"My fascination with polyphony and European music began very early, while I was having classical piano lessons, and also playing all kinds of music with my cousins as a child in a family band. My most wonderful discovery from that time was when I first heard Bach. Albuquerque, New Mexico, where I grew up, had a surprising amount of music, and I had access to much of it, as well as a large number of visiting musicians. I remember Paderewski coming to play there on one of his final tours of the United States.

"Deciding to record Bach's music myself, though, wasn't my idea. It was the brainchild of a friend of mine at Philips in Japan, Mr Koyama. I didn't really want to do it at first, not least because so many other artists have specialized in that repertoire. His idea, I think, was for me to play the music as written, but I said that if I was going to do it, I'd want to do it my way and introduce some jazz improvisation. They agreed, but only if I played the whole thing entirely as an unaccompanied soloist. The project took me a couple of years, and I had to go back and reaquaint myself with all the preludes and fugues, some of which I hadn't played at all, and others I hadn't touched since I was a child."

So to end with, as we had got round to discussing the music of Bach, I couldn't resist asking John what he thought about his good friend Loussier's quip. He laughed a lot, but then he got serious. "At the heart of it, he's wrong. And that's because my real passion has been jazz, and I've had the good fortune to watch it develop since the 1920s. I've seen at first hand the search for a language that could express more than simple emotions, and it's been a wonderful journey being able to observe this. For me the real importance hasn't been so much to do with my playing, but watching the entire development of jazz into a great art."

18 jacques loussier

When I was still a small boy, studying the piano and taking my first steps as a classical cellist, Jacques Loussier's original *Play Bach Trio* discs on the London label, with their starkly abstract covers, and the blotchy photographs on the reverse of Loussier himself, Pierre Michelot and Christian Garros, made their way into the house. I played them until they were worn out. In common with a lot of European enthusiasts for both jazz and the classics, for me there was something immediately appealing about these LPs that brought the two worlds together. I little suspected then that I would eventually get to know Jacques well, that we would spend time together in France, and work on several short films and a BBC radio series. I have written Jacques' liner notes for the best part of the last decade, and been present in the studio for the recording of several of his albums. This piece draws together articles written at various times for *Jazziz* and *Piano*.

In the early 1980s, living in a hidden valley so deep in the countryside of Provence that there was virtually no sound of twentieth-century life apart from the odd tractor or water pump, Jacques Loussier set his mind to electronic composition and running a recording studio. For the previous twenty years, he had been one of the most popular jazz pianists in Europe, after setting up his Play Bach Trio in 1959, and, despite the disapproval of most critics, building up a massive following in his native France, as well as Britain, Germany and Japan, playing jazz versions of the music of Johann Sebastian Bach.

Although he was barely known outside Europe and Japan, with close on six million album sales in those territories matched by little more than a hundred thousand in the United States, he was playing over one hundred and fifty sold-out concerts a year at the likes of the Salle Pleyel in Paris, or London's Royal Festival Hall, and in 1979 he decided to call it a day while he was still ahead of the game.

His years in seclusion, surrounded by his own vineyards and olive groves in the valley of Miraval, were hardly wasted. He produced film scores, classical concerti, and electro-acoustic pieces such as *Pulsions* or *Lumières*, which acquired a cult following in France. Meanwhile the studio which he had converted from a massive sheep-shearing shed flourished, and Loussier would emerge from his house to find the members of Wham! or Pink Floyd stretched out on the lawns outside the control room as they worked on their latest album. One day, Elton John flew in from Nice for the afternoon to patch in some lyrics, and before long plenty of other rock musicians began to book an annual session there, where the cordon bleu gastronomy and excellent products of the estate's vineyards were matched by quaint accommodation converted from a Victorian water tower, with breathtaking views of unspoilt countryside.

What changed everything for Loussier was the Bach tercentenary in 1985. Invited to form a trio to celebrate the composer with whom he was so closely identified, Loussier found his new companions, bassist Vincent Charbonnier and drummer André Arpino so convivial, and their music such a quantum leap forward from his old trio, that he went back on the road. And although he has not quite gone back to the number of concerts he was playing in the 1970s, he has kept up a full touring schedule ever since. But the music itself has changed a lot since the 1950s.

When he started out, Loussier was a brilliant student of the Paris Conservatoire, and widely tipped to become one of France's leading clas-

Jacques Loussier (left), Benoit Dunoyer de Segonzac and André Arpino (Telarc)

sical recitalists. He financed his student years by playing all the music that Parisian nightlife had to offer a jobbing pianist, everything from gipsy songs to cabaret chansons, and for a while he accompanied such legends as Charles Aznavour, while continuing his classical studies. But then something that had begun as a hobby took over his life.

"There was a piano in the place where we had our lunch at the Conservatoire," he told me. "And most days, my fellow students would say to me, 'Come on Jacques, play your Bach to us!' Because I had begun to realize that Bach's music was ideal for jazz improvisation. So many of the structures are similar, with patterns of sixteen or thirty-two measures, and the left-hand parts are often very similar to jazz basslines. So I would give the jazz treatment to something from the 'Forty-eight,' or the *Anna Magdelena Notebook*, and they'd all crowd round the piano and urge me on. I started the first trio in order to make an album to amuse my friends at the Conservatoire. I had no idea it would catch on."

But catch on it did, and between 1959 and 1963 Loussier recorded four best-selling albums for the London label. There was a weekly show on prime-time British television, and similar media interest in France. His bassist Pierre Michelot had been in Bud Powell's famous Paris trio with Kenny Clarke, and drummer Christian Garros was also well-known in the city. Some of their earliest discs became European classics, including *Air On A G-string* which has been used to advertise Hamlet cigars ever since. But the trio's sense of time, and Loussier's improvisations, were still firmly rooted in the French bebop tradition, the style fostered by such long-term Paris residents as the American *émigrés* Powell, Clarke or Nathan Davis. It took the much more open approach of Loussier's "new" trio of the 1980s to explore such unfamiliar territory as Latin beats, rock rhythms and modal harmonies.

This wider stylistic range, and the change in Loussier's own approach to the piano during the time he worked as a composer, altered the sound of his group completely. His sensitive classical touch is unchanged, but, for the first time, the influence of the jazz musicians he listened to and admired, men such as Keith Jarrett and John Lewis, could be heard in his playing, and in the mid-1990s Loussier took a bold step and began experimenting with jazz versions of composers other than Bach.

"Each of them presents a different challenge," he told me, on a sunny afternoon outside Miraval in 1996, as he worked on recording the first of these new arrangements, Vivaldi's *Four Seasons*. "When I do an arrangement, I look at the music and try to decide which part will still be played in a classical style, where I can open it up for jazz improvisation, and where I'll introduce some freer sections for myself or the bassist. Vivaldi's music is very different from Bach's in terms of its structure. There is jazz already present in Bach, in the number of measures, his harmonies, and so on, but Vivaldi may stay on one chord for many measures, and he may choose not to develop a harmonic idea. He often repeats a single theme several times, but in his string orchestrations he alters the tone colour. I had to approach the *Four Seasons* in terms of light and colour, and to think how to change these for my jazz improvisations."

Soon, the crystalline charm of his version of *Winter*, with its icy triangle effects, and the sweeping breezy soundscape of *Summer* had become part of his concert programmes.

Loussier is quick to defend the charge that he bases his jazz on other people's music rather than creating his own. He is, after all, famous for producing jazz versions of Bach, and so to some extent his public expect him to "swing" the classics, but he feels firstly that this is source material every bit as rewarding for the improviser as playing standards, and secondly, as he has progressed over the last couple of years with his investigation of his French heritage, Satie, Ravel and Debussy, he has slipped many of his own compositions onto the albums. The *Nympheas* variations, which appear on his Ravel disc alongside *Bolero*, are a set of his own pieces, part composed-part improvised, inspired by Monet's waterlily paintings, and there is a similar type of new composition mixed in among Satie's *Gnossiennes* and *Gymnopédies*.

In 1998, Vincent Charbonnier, still in his mid-thirties, suffered a massive stroke, and has been unable to play since, but his replacement in the trio, Benoit Dunoyer de Segonzac, has kept Charbonnier's spirit of openness and exploration alive. I hooked up with this version of the group in 2000 when they were in Paris to record their disc of Debussy arrangements, and Loussier was bubbling with enthusiasm. "Right now, I think the trio is exactly as I want it. We think and play as if we were a single person. I only have to hint at an idea and Benoit or André can take it up immediately. Although we play so many concerts, and the public expects to hear certain pieces like *Air On A G-string*, we change what we do far more from night to night. And also, playing the music of French composers has given me a much greater stylistic range."

I wondered if his affection for Debussy had been kindled in the 1950s by his tutor at the Paris Conservatoire, Yves Nat, who was himself a protégé of the great composer, but Jacques assured me this was no case of apostolic succession.

"Ever since I began playing piano, I was drawn to the music of Debussy and Ravel and their contemporary French composers," he recalled. "But the particular thing that attracted me so greatly to Debussy, and which

made me want to do these new interpretations is the beauty of his harmonies. In almost all the pieces, there's a sequence of harmonies where
each one creates a new effect, and the challenge for the improviser is to
work with these. They can be restrictive for a pianist, simply in terms of
the number of notes you have to play in each chord to achieve the cor-
rect harmonic effect. This gets even more problematic in creating trio
arrangements from his orchestral pieces, such as *Prélude à l'aprés midi
d'un faune*. With just the piano to recreate those complex orchestral harmonies, it feels sometimes as if you need twenty-five fingers! But then
of course I have the bass as well because Benoit can help in creating the
harmonies."

So, I wondered, does he tackle creating a jazz interpretation of
Debussy in the same way as he has gone about dealing with the works of
Bach? Surely the keyboard technique alone is dramatically different?

"Yes, that's true. You can't create a watery texture by attacking the
keyboard in the same way as you would a piece of baroque music. Just
the same considerations apply in creating a jazz interpretation of Debussy
as they would in performing the music as it was written, in a classical
context.

"When I started listening hard to *Prélude à l'aprés midi d'un faune*, I
didn't think about trying to recreate the orchestration precisely. I was
more concerned with the feeling of the piece, but by simply looking at
a reduction of the score I saw immediately that there were possibilities for adding elements of jazz, with bass and drums, in a section that
follows that very familiar introduction that everyone knows so well,
with its haunting flute melody. The challenge for the trio is to match
the atmosphere created by the orchestra, and to make the manner of
improvisation appropriate. The pleasure in doing this is to find a way
to produce the same colour, the same joy, so that someone listening to
the CD will experience some of the same emotions as in hearing the
orchestral version.

"With the piano pieces like *Clair de lune*, there's a different problem. You just can't add bass and drums and a jazzy treatment anywhere
you like. The opening of the piece is dreamlike, and just not appropriate for such an approach, which might kill its spirit. But the second
theme is a different matter, and its melody and underlying harmonies
lend themselves very readily to jazz. So that's where we've opened it up
for improvisation, before coming back to the original piece, much as
Debussy wrote it."

Those who know Debussy's music well might be startled by the gospel rhythm that creeps in to *La fille aux cheveux de lin*, or the similarly

vernacular feel of *L'isle joyeuse,* but they will find familiar textures in the luminous, transparent feel of the *Arabesque,* with its beautiful upper register bass solo.

Most of my meetings with Jacques seem to involve some kind of gastronomic experience, and, as we savoured the last drops of a rather good claret, Jacques stared at his empty plate, and reflected on my question about the difference in trying to make convincing jazz out of Debussy compared to Bach. "Well," he said at last. "When I play Bach, I think of a little saucisson and a glass of red wine, but when I play Debussy, I am surrounded by water. And if you listen to *La Cathedral Engloutie,* a piece we all know from studying the piano, you can hear that Benoit and I are exploring something completely new in my music – the darkness of the twilight depths."

At first glance, Debussy might seem an unlikely subject for a jazz album, but, as Jacques pointed out, his influence is widely felt in jazz from Bix Beiderbecke to Bill Evans, so why not, for a change, bring jazz to impressionism, rather than the other way round?

19 junior mance

I've always had a soft spot for the blues-drenched playing of Junior Mance, whose work I got to know in considerable detail as I was researching *Groovin' High*, and listened to his many discs with Dizzy Gillespie and his contemporaneous playing for Cannonball Adderley. We'd met when he visited the UK with Lionel Hampton's Golden Men of Jazz, in 1992, and I presented their concert in what was then the very newly-opened environment of Symphony Hall in Birmingham. He'd sat at the piano comping for Hampton's two-fingered piano during the soundcheck, and on the concert itself was not only a splendid member of the rhythm team along with bassist Jimmy Woode and drummer Bobby Durham, but turned in some highly attractive solos. This interview was carried out during a visit to New York in the late 1990s, and appeared in the March 2002 edition of *Piano*.

During February 2002, one of the legendary pianists of modern jazz, Junior Mance, made a lengthy UK tour. His personal, highly distinctive style, blending the phrasing and soulfulness of the blues with the harmonies of bebop, is immediately recognizable, and, as I discovered, it has its roots in his upbringing, in the city of Chicago.

His father was a pianist, and so was the father of the first bandleader with whom Junior, whose given name is Julian, worked at the age of seventeen, saxophonist Gene Ammons – son of the great boogie-woogie player Albert Ammons.

"That was my first gig," laughed Junior, "and that's when I learned what real heavy serious jazz was all about. I stayed with Gene a long time, and not only did I have my first working experience as a professional with him, but also my first recording experience, on the discs we made together for several labels including Savoy and Prestige. I'd been playing in a college big band in Chicago when I was just out of high school and that's where I met Gene and he offered me that job. One thing that stands out in my memory about Gene was he had an incredible knack for

Junior Mance (right) sharing the keyboard with Lionel Hampton,
Symphony Hall, Birmingham, 1992 (Derek Drescher)

reading music. He could look at a piece once, and because he had a photographic memory he'd immediately have the whole thing in his head. That meant he could concentrate straight away on things like phrasing and making a piece swing. In a big band, although he'd be playing tenor, even the lead alto player would follow Gene's phrasing because he was such an exceptional player."

Junior went on to work alongside several other great saxophonists, the first of them being Sonny Stitt, who came into the line-up alongside Gene Ammons. "For a time Gene augmented his band, first to a sextet with Sonny Stitt, and then he added a couple of trumpets and a trombone. Gene played tenor, but Sonny played an instrument that he's very rarely been featured on, the baritone sax, doubling between that and the alto. But for solo playing, Stitt would pick up the tenor, and he'd go head to head with Gene on what they used to call 'tenor battles,' where they both tried to outblow each other."

Junior worked on several record sessions with Stitt, and then went on to spend a year and a half with the tenor saxophonist Lester Young. With his light, airy phrasing, and his eccentric personality that mixed a withdrawn diffidence with an earthy sense of humour, Young was a fascinating personality.

"We never rehearsed, and Lester, or 'Pres' as we called him, believed in everybody getting the chance to play. People used to ask him why he gave us so many solos when he was supposed to be the star himself. And he would say, 'We might play somewhere where the people don't like me, and they might like one of the other guys in the band more.' As a consequence it was a really fun band because you couldn't look upon Lester as a leader. It was more like having a jam session every night, and we'd all say 'Hey! Let's play!'"

Junior met the next of his great saxophone colleagues after he'd been conscripted into the services. "Because I didn't play a marching instrument, they wouldn't let me join an army band. So, one night I was doing guard duty and I heard this fabulous music coming from the building I was pacing around, the services club. I had to walk around it with my rifle for two hours, and then I got an hour's break. So as soon as I got off duty, I hurried upstairs in the club, and there was Cannonball Adderley, playing with an army big band. It was so good I thought it was someone playing records, but it was a real live group. I hadn't been near a piano during the few months I'd been in the army, only guns, but I did something I never do, and asked Cannonball if I could sit in. The band were all in sharp civilian suits, and here I was with my helmet and combat boots, but the piano player recognized me, reached down, grabbed my arm and pulled me up on stage. The band were all giving me disdainful looks, but their pianist disappeared as soon as I got there. So they called for a Count Basie tune, and after they'd played the intro, Cannonball threw me a solo. Well, I didn't want to wear out my welcome, so I kinda stopped after about three choruses, and looked up, and all the heads in the band were nodding, and Cannonball shouted, 'Yeah, play some more!' So I just stretched out. After the set, Cannonball said, 'So who are you?'

"I said 'Junior Mance.'

"He said, 'Oh yeah, if you're Junior Mance what are you doing here?'

"I looked at him and said, 'If it comes to that, what are *you* doing here?'

"And then he laughed because he had just about all my records with Sonny Stitt. And, to cut a long story short, he pulled some strings with the army, and wangled me into his band. And I like to think he saved my life because just about all the rest of the infantry company I was with got wiped out in Korea."

After they both left the army, Junior went on to work with Cannonball for several years. When Cannonball broke up his own band and went off to join Miles Davis, Junior went to Dizzy Gillespie's band, and it was through Dizzy that he met the entrepreneur Norman Granz and began his career as a solo pianist. Since then he's seldom looked back, and he's playing as well now as he was during the many years when he played elegant piano and bass duets in New York bars such as the Cookery or Bradley's, or during the time in the early 1990s when he took to the road with Lionel Hampton's Golden Men of Jazz.

20 marian mcpartland

In the world of jazz broadcasting, Marian McPartland is greatly admired by all of us who have tried our hand at presenting in front of a microphone. Her National Public Radio show, *Piano Jazz*, celebrated twenty-five years of continuous broadcasting in 2004, and during its run Marian has interviewed and duetted with just about everyone who is anyone in the world of jazz. She won a special Grammy award in the 2004 ceremony in recognition of her outstanding services to music. She and I have broadcast together several times, and I have occasionally attended the taping of her show, which is always an object lesson in focus, unflappability and good humour in the face of everything that technology, the weather, or fickle guests can throw at it. As a publisher, I have long been trying to persuade Marian to pick up her pen again and write her memoirs, to follow in the wake of her excellent collection of short essays, *All In Good Time*. To date, apart from the occasional autobiographical liner note, she has resisted the challenge. Maybe this previously unpublished interview, which took place late in 1999, will prompt her to expand her recollections?

Elegant as always, Marian McPartland stepped from her car into the lobby of my hotel in downtown Manhattan, and, as all English folk are prone to do in the middle of the afternoon, we set about finding a decent pot of tea. Once it arrived, we settled down to talk. Although the vista below us swept across the Hudson River towards New Jersey, with Ellis Island and its long association with new arrivals to the United States just visible to our left, our conversation started not on the topic of Marian's adopted home of America, but back in pre-war Britain, where she had gone on the road in her younger days with the pianist, composer and entertainer Billy Mayerl.

"I was at the Guildhall School of Music," she smiled, "allegedly studying to be a concert pianist, but in fact I was already so into jazz that playing classical music just got in the way. For some unknown reason, I decided to go and see Billy at his studio. I think this was because to me,

Marian McPartland and young admirers, London, 1996 (Derek Drescher)

as a student, he was sort of a jazz person. Not totally, but he played what I thought of then as nice jazzy pieces. I went over there and I seem to remember one reason was that I wanted him to show me some better chords. I guess he did, but the next thing out of his mouth was that he was going to hire me for this group he was in the process of forming to take out on the road. It was a four-piano act.

"Of course I was very thrilled and said I would like to go. My parents were horrified. They didn't exactly disown me, or throw me out of the house, but my father offered me £1000 not to go, and that was pretty good money in those days.

"Anyway, I said no to the money. So Daddy decided he'd come up and see Billy, and ask him all the important questions: 'What do you have in mind for my daughter? Will she be in safe hands? How much money is she going to earn?' He can't have been a particularly good bargainer because I think I ended up getting £5 a week.

"This was in the late thirties, and the whole experience was very interesting because he had the four of us learn our music by ear. Billy allocated all of us parts to play around his own playing. We did a lot of his compositions, of course, as well as popular songs of the day like *The Bells Of St. Mary's* or novelty pieces by Raymond Scott, and light classics such as Jessel's *Parade Of The Tin Soldiers.*

"On stage it was pretty spectacular because we had gold pianos. He played a grand, and then the other three of us had uprights. He had these marvellous outfits made for me and Kathleen Hepple, who were the two girls in the act, and the other male pianist, who was equally well-kitted out, was George Middleton. The first date we played was in Norwich. In those days there were variety theatres or music halls all around the country, and this opening date was at the Norwich Empire. From there, we went on to appear all over the place. I think I must've played in every music hall or variety theatre in Britain, good or bad."

I wondered if this could possibly have been a profitable venture, not least because of lugging the four pianos around the length and breadth of the land, while trying to keep them reasonably in tune.

"I think it was the Challen music company, the manufacturers, who supplied the instruments," Marian recalled. "Maybe in one or two places they supplied pianos from a local store, but by and large we always appeared with the golden pianos. To be honest, I wasn't too worried about those practicalities. I was like a kid in a candy store because I was in show business, and although my parents didn't like it, they didn't stop me from doing it."

Did this continue into the early years of World War Two?

"Billy broke up the group a few months before the war began. When it started, I was doing concert parties for a group at the pier theatre in Felixstowe. Things suddenly got very ominous, when one day men started putting up barbed wire on the beach. My sister was there with me, and we both knew something horrible was going to happen. So I left there, but I kept playing and joined a variety troupe called Carroll Levis and his Discoveries. They'd been looking for a pianist, and although I wasn't exactly a 'discovery,' I became his piano player for the whole show. I would rehearse the pit band for every new act, and once again it was back to the theatre circuit. I think the first date with Carroll was the Nottingham Empire. There'd be a juggler, a dancer and a singer, and then I'd play some selection on the piano. I did that for quite a while."

Had it been during her travels with Levis that she'd first met Jimmy McPartland, when he came to Europe with the American forces?

"I didn't meet him when he was in Britain," she said. "Although I think his first posting was somewhere in Wales. But while he was there, my call-up papers arrived, instructing me to join the army. There was an alternative, which allowed me to continue being an entertainer, so I joined ENSA [the Entertainments National Service Association]. But soon afterwards I met one of my former colleagues from Carroll Levis's group, and she said to me I should join USO [the United Service Organization] instead. 'It's much better, they pay more, and you'll meet all these lovely American guys.'

"So that's what I did. I joined USO, and I was with the first group that went over after the invasion in 1944. When we landed we were so close behind the invading forces that we had to wade ashore and put up tents, using the same kind of mess-tins and eating the same food as the GIs. We gradually made our way through all these battered and broken towns in northern France, and we finally arrived in Belgium in a place called Eupen. That's where I met Jimmy, whom I soon found out had been part of a gun crew, working in a gun emplacement. One of our group, a man called Willie Shaw, was from Chicago, and he pulled strings to get Jimmy out of combat and into special service, 'This man should be playing his horn! He shouldn't be operating a gun!'

"Lo and behold, Jimmy appeared. Actually, Jimmy was one person I hadn't managed to hear about in England. I had records by people like Sidney Bechet, Bud Freeman, Benny Goodman and Art Tatum, just about everybody it seemed. But somehow I had missed out on Jimmy, and didn't know who he was. But he was obviously something special because word was going round the camp: 'Jimmy McPartland's coming! Jimmy McPartland's going to play!'

"They organized a big jam session for Jimmy, and I wanted to get in on it, which I managed to do. And so I played at the jam session. Years later, Jimmy said, 'I saw you coming in that tent and thought to myself, here comes a woman piano player and she wants to play, and she's going to be terrible. And you were!'

"I don't think I was quite that bad, but I suppose I didn't keep time too well in those days! But he must have liked me because not long afterwards they put us together to play in a group that went out every day to entertain troops in the front lines. There'd be Jimmy, me, a clarinet player from the USO show and a GI bassist and drummer. There were a couple of other acts, including a girl who swallowed razor blades. Believe it or not, that was her act. And we'd set off at the crack of dawn, with me dressed up in beads and sequins to please the GIs, and in some places there'd be a stage for us, and in others we'd have to perform on the back of a truck. Meanwhile we would sometimes get caught in air raids. Nothing terrible ever happened to us, but we had some near misses.

"Then Jimmy started to run a band at the hotel in Eupen, which was a rest area for the officers. All the USO personnel lived in this hotel, which was called the Schmidtsroth. It's terrible to say it, but although this awful war was going on all round us because Eupen wasn't far from the Battle of the Bulge or the Battle of the Ardennes, we were having a really good time. It was one of those things. There we were, and I suppose it was a matter of what you might call propinquity: we fell in love, or lust, or both, and we arranged to get married. Jimmy's commanding officer said to me, 'You shouldn't get married! You haven't known him long enough.' However we begged and pleaded. So in February of 1945 we got married in Aachen, Germany, in a military government building. Jimmy's CO was very kind, and arranged a car to take us to Brussels for our honeymoon, where we stayed for a week.

"When we got back, the blow fell. Jimmy had to go back to his outfit, and I was sent to Paris to join another show, so for a while things were pretty hectic, until we could meet up again."

This prompted me to ask what on earth Marian's parents, the Turners, made of her marriage. After all, if her father had been prepared to buy her off from playing with Billy Mayerl, this must have come as an even bigger shock to the system.

"They were always worried that I would marry the wrong person," Marian grinned, somewhat conspiratorially. "Somebody who wasn't 'top drawer.' For instance, my mother would say, 'I don't know what'll become of you! You'll marry a musician and live in an attic!' And, of course, in some respects that's exactly what happened, but I didn't tell them at the time because I thought they'd come rushing over to the Continent to try to put a stop to it. Of course, they found out later because Jimmy's CO, who was so nice and had been so kind to us, went over to England and arranged to meet my father for lunch. He broke the news that I was married. He told me afterwards that my father took it very well, but my mother didn't, and that she had cried all day. Eventually we went over there, and the two of them really fell for Jimmy. He was very charming and this won over my mother. She took me aside and said, 'Oh! He's not a bit like an American! He's so polite!'"

I've always had a soft spot for the discs that Marian and Jimmy made in Britain for Carlo Krahmer's Esquire label. Was it on this visit to meet her parents that they'd cut such spirited records as *China Boy* or *Blues For Carlo*?

"No, I think that was later.[1] We did come over to England a couple of times, and we made a few informal recordings, mainly done at somebody's house. After we were married and went to the States, we made some more records. But this is jumping ahead a bit. Jimmy left the army and joined USO while he was still in Europe. In due course we went to New York together, and, while we were there, he was offered a job to play at Condon's because Wild Bill Davison was leaving. But, on that occasion,

Jimmy turned Eddie down because he wanted to go to Chicago to see his family, and that's what we did.

"I think that what were more or less our first American recordings are ones we did ourselves in Chicago. We made two records which we sold to a company called Harmony Records. The four sides included *Royal Garden Blues* and a number Jimmy wrote called *The Daughter Of Sister Kate*. Then we recorded again on one of our trips to England, and the results of those, with Freddy Gardner, came out on Harmony as well."

To me, Marian and Jimmy's recordings from that period had a very attractive joyous quality about them. What did Marian think accounted for this?

"I think a lot of the joy comes from having had the opportunity to play during the war to audiences who were really enjoying it. It was a fantastic experience to play to thousands of people in a field. They'd throw up a stage made out of little more than a few rough boards, and I'd play an army-style gray-painted upright piano, which somehow or other they managed to deliver to the area, and which was even kept in tune. Throughout that time, Jimmy was playing really well, and so it was huge fun.

"I remember while we were still in Eupen, before we were married, there was going to be a big concert, but the hotel piano had seen better days. So Jimmy and a group of his pals went round to the house of a well-known German sympathizer who lived in the town and liberated her piano. She got a piece of paper from the adjutant saying the piano would be returned to her after the war. She followed them into the street wringing her hands, but they took it, and put it up on stage. That was the final *coup de grâce* when it came to making up my mind about Jimmy. Anyone who would go to those lengths to get me a decent piano had to be a man worth marrying! I was glad he insisted on a piano because when I'd originally gone out there I'd been warned that there may not be any pianos, and so I had learned the accordion. As it turned out, in the vast American army, just miles from the front line there were enlisted piano tuners! Which is just as well because I wasn't a particularly good accordionist and could just about comp my way through a few tunes. In the end I never had to play it once."

When Marian and Jimmy reached his home town of Chicago, I was interested to discover whether Marian felt there was a contrast between what she found, and the privations that everyone in England had gone through, with rationing and 'making do.'

"I don't think people in Chicago, even now, know what it is to be deprived of anything. They've never been in a real war. They don't know about getting one egg a month, not being able to order a steak, having to drink powdered milk, or anything like that. I used to wonder what would happen if people in the United States were faced with that, year in year out, as we had been in England. But, of course, when I got there I just loved Chicago, and still do.

"Jimmy had been away for so long that he was not immediately in the swing of things. We stayed with his family for a while. I should mention that Jimmy was a pretty heavy drinker in those days, although he subsequently joined AA which was a great relief, but a huge amount of drinking went on as he met up again with all his friends and relations. Before long, I just wanted to get to work, to play somewhere, and within a short time that's what happened. We opened at a place called the Rose Bowl, which was a glorified bowling alley with a bar on the other side. It was not really the greatest date in the world, but, nevertheless, we opened there with a quintet: Jimmy and me, Lew Finnerty on drums, Ben Carlton on bass, and Lou Renear was the clarinet player.

"At that time, Jimmy was so proud of me and everything I could do. I'd play a piano solo in the middle of the set, but I was kind of dumb, and I'd play something like *Clair de lune*, and the minute I'd start to play, someone would get a strike in the bowling alley and what I was playing would be drowned out by everyone shouting 'Whoa, yeah!' It wasn't exactly the best time for me to be playing a piano solo."

How had Marian put this early experience to use, when she arrived in New York a few years later and started appearing with her own trio on 52nd Street?

"Getting there had a lot to do with Jimmy. He was such a booster for me, and he kept saying, 'You shouldn't be playing in my group, you should have your own!' And in due course I did start my own trio, but to start with I continued to play with him.

When we moved to New York, I think we'd played in just about every dive in Chicago, as well as all the better clubs like the Blue Note. On the way to New York, our first gig was at a club in Philadelphia called the Rendezvous, and it's one of those odd things about this musician's life, but it was then that I started to meet jazz legends on level terms. In our band there was Wilber de Paris on trombone, and one night he took a night off and his brother Sidney came and played in Wilber's place, doing two-cornet things with Jimmy. That was our first stop in the East. Then we settled in Long Island for a while.

"We'd go to hear a lot of jazz in Manhattan, and ended up going frequently to the Embers which was just a couple of blocks away from 52nd Street. I wanted to hear people I'd only known about through recordings in England, and particularly the women musicians, like Mary Lou Williams and Cleo Brown. At the time we arrived in New York, Joe Bushkin played regularly at the Embers, and he had a big and loyal public that turned up to support him. As he played, he'd half turn to face the crowd, then he'd stick his right leg out, fix his eye on somebody, and he'd move about at the piano, more or less flirting with the audience. He was still doing much the same when he appeared on my radio show in about 1998. At the Embers, he drew in celebrities like Tallulah Bankhead, and other big names of the time.

"Anyway in due course, Joe left, and I went in there with a trio to replace him. I had great musicians: Don Lamond on drums and Eddie Safranski on bass. The group opposite me was led by Eddie Heywood, who was not particularly well-known at the time, and, of course, I was a real unknown. And, needless to say, business was not very good. When Joe Bushkin left, his followers had gone with him, and neither of us had the same degree of fame or loyal audience. To cap it all, Eddie had a slight stammer, which didn't put the audience at ease when he was talking. As a result, Ralph Watkins, the owner of the club, decided he had to do something to increase business, so he hired a couple of extra guests, which was a big thrill for me because they were Roy Eldridge and Coleman Hawkins.

"Now, for some reason, Eddie refused to play with them. Needless to say, particularly because my trio was the second group on the bill, I was absolutely thrilled to work with two such giants. They were so nice to me, too. Roy always talked about it until his dying day, telling people what a good time he'd had during that period at the Embers. They must have been satisfied with my playing too because there was no breaking off to discuss chords or things that they thought I was getting wrong. We just played, and I suppose after my years in Chicago I knew most of the songs anyhow.

"The main thing I remember was that I was still very green and callow when it came to speaking on the microphone. I was so nervous that I had to write down on a piece of paper what I was going to say! I only had to thank the audience and introduce Eddie Heywood. Nowadays, as listeners to *Piano Jazz* will know, you can hardly stop me talking, but in those days it was really hard for me to say anything in public. On top of that, there was a live broadcast once a week from the Embers, presented by Jazzbo Collins. During the show, Jazzbo would talk to me, and I would answer him in a very faint voice, but that was the beginning of my radio career!"

Although Marian played for quite some time at the Embers, the club that she is most associated with from that period in the 1950s was the Hickory House. How did that connection begin?

"I think we moved there quite soon after that first period at the Embers. I was working through Joe Glaser's agency, and when the booking came in, somebody at the office said to me, 'Marian, if you play your cards right, you can maybe stay at the Hickory House for three or four months.' So we opened there, with a drummer named Mel Zelnick and Max Wayne from Chicago on bass.

"It was a great success, and nobody at the club ever said anything about leaving. The months went by, and different people came and went in the trio. Mousie Alexander came in on drums, and finally he was replaced by Joe Morello, and we had Vinnie Burke on bass. Not long ago Savoy records reissued the Hickory House recordings by that trio from 1953. Then Vinnie left and Bill Crow came in, and for me that was really the definitive trio from that period."

Marian's pen portrait of Joe Morello in her book *All In Good Time* paints a picture of a very close musical relationship between them. Did she still see it in those terms?

"It was, and it still is, close. I love Joe. He's a wonderful person, very warm, very funny, and I think he played as well as he's ever played with me in those days. Don't forget he was with me for the best part of four years. Eventually he started to get offers from elsewhere, but it was Bill who left first, to go with Gerry Mulligan. Joe stayed on, despite offers from the Dorsey Brothers and Stan Kenton, who invited him even though they were worried that his eyesight was so bad he might not be able to read the music. His intuition and his ear were so quick that of course he'd have done very well with any of those groups, or with Benny Goodman who also offered him a job. Anyway he still didn't go, until I took time off for a short trip home to England. When I came back I found that Dave Brubeck had made him an offer.

"I'm still mad at Dave! He and Paul Desmond used to come into the club quite often while we were there, and I'd think how nice it was of them to come down and listen. But they were really there to see what they thought about Joe. Of course, he had to leave, even though things were going well for him with my trio because he was getting awards, we appeared on the *Tonight* show and we made at least two albums for Capitol during that Hickory House period. So, anyhow, he went with Dave, and I had several changes, most of them becoming really good rhythm sections. There was Ben Tucker and Dave Bailey, and then Steve Swallow and Pete LaRoca, which was wild! Pete's such a great drummer. He went off to be a lawyer, but his playing was, as I say, wild. He'd go over barlines in his solos, and you really had to know what you were doing to stay with him."

Talking of drummers, I recalled Jake Hanna mentioning his time with Marian when I spoke to him during one of his regular English tours in the mid-1990s.

"We had a lot of fun, at the Hickory House, in Florida and on the road. Jake's got a great sense of humour, and he's also a wonderful drummer, and played very well indeed with me, as you can hear on our Concord records from the early 1980s, with a bassist called Steve LaSpina. I had so many wonderful members of the trio during the years, and it's still going on. A few weeks from now I'm going to Chicago and I'll be playing with Jim Cox on bass and Phil Gratteau on drums, who I really love working with."

We then went off at a tangent about the myriad of bassists and drummers who have worked with Marian, but we got back to the serious point, exemplified by Swallow and LaRoca, that Marian has never been categorizable as a "mainstream" or "traditional" pianist. She's always had an ear firmly cocked towards the new and the exciting, from Ornette to Coltrane and beyond.

"I think that's because I've never wanted to be perceived as a fuddy-duddy, or just to be 'stuck' in one style. I'm so interested in what goes on, I just want to try it. Steve and Pete were at the cutting edge of the time and I had to be, too. I first heard Steve when he was with Benny Goodman before he joined me, and we've stayed in touch ever since. Only a year or so ago he and Carla Bley were my guests on *Piano Jazz*. Back in the days when he was in my trio, Steve was playing the double bass, of course. I remember him saying something that I've since had the chance to tease him about whenever we meet because he said, 'I'll never play an electric bass!' Of course he's made quite a name for himself on the bass guitar since then!"

We then moved on to thinking about some of the other musicians with whom Steve played in his early days, notably Bud Freeman, the Chicagoan tenorist. And then, by way of various other musicians' names, our conversation looped back to Marian's interest in hearing other female jazz instrumentalists when she arrived in the United States. First among them was Mary Lou Williams, whom Marian has not only written about in her book, but celebrated in an album of her music for Concord.

"When Jimmy and I first came to New York, it was hard to find her, but eventually we discovered she was working in a little club called the Downbeat. I went over between sets and talked to her. She was quite friendly, and we subsequently worked together briefly. That was in a place called the Composer Room, during one of my breaks from the Hickory House, and my trio was featured opposite hers. It was a kick working opposite her. Years later she played at the Cookery, but, in between, for some reason or another she got mad at me. Maybe it was because I had a long residency at the Carlyle Hotel, and she became jealous or something, but whenever I'd go down to hear her, she'd be very cool and offputting. This went on for quite a while.

"Also when we arrived in the city, it had been equally difficult to find out where Cleo Brown was because, as I eventually found out, she'd become a Jehovah's Witness in Denver. Some years later, I asked a friend of mine down there to go and see her and ask if she'd come on my radio show, which she did. What I'd liked most about her old records, which I used to listen to a lot, were her charming, witty, slightly coquettish songs, but when she came on *Piano Jazz* she'd got religion and she refused to sing any of those old numbers. Everything she did had a religious point to it, but the woman could not stop swinging. That was something she couldn't hide! All her music had a bluesy tinge to it, and we managed to make quite a decent show of it in the end."

Marian's now such a consummate broadcaster, and the way she described making the Cleo Brown show into a good programme for the radio perfectly reinforces this, that she makes me wonder what had happened to the shy tongue-tied girl who had to write down all her announcements at the Embers.

"It took me quite a while, but Jimmy was a role model for me because he was always wonderful on the microphone. He'd say to me, 'Be yourself!' It was easier said than done, but I learned by doing, particularly during all those years at the Hickory House. Then some time before *Piano Jazz*, I went to a radio station in Manhattan called WBAI, a Pacifica station which meant they didn't pay any money, but I offered to do a radio programme because there wasn't enough jazz being heard on the air. So I'd go there and play all kinds of records from Benny Goodman and Maynard Ferguson to Ornette Coleman. It was there that I started to do interviews, and that got me into the feeling of being able to interview people. So when I started *Piano Jazz* I felt pretty confident. But I made a big mistake by having Mary Lou as a first guest. I think the jealousy I described earlier came to a head, and she felt I was putting one over on her by having my own show. She told the producer, 'I should be doing this show!' The producer calmed her down and told her she was the guest of honour. And that mollified her a bit, but she was still not in a good frame of mind.

"At one point she played something, and I said, 'Oh, I really like that chord.' I played it back to her, and she said, 'I didn't play that!' She wasn't going to give me any help. I stumbled and stuttered, but she gradually got better, relaxed into it, and at the end she was enjoying it so much that she sang a song. Afterwards we all went to the Russian Tea Room, and then the producer took us all to dinner. By then, she had quite recovered from her pique, and we remained friendly until the end of her life. I used to send her stuff regularly to Durham, where she was teaching at Duke University. That's where she wrote her big religious pieces, and not long ago we did one, *Mary Lou's Mass*, at Washington National Cathedral, a gorgeous building, in which there were two choirs. Mary-Ann Brownlow from Borders bookshop in Washington fundraised and helped stage it, Carmen Lundy sang the solos, David Baker conducted, and Frank Tate and I went down to play with a little jazz group mainly made up of local Washington players. It was really splendid."

By then the dusk had drawn in over the river, lights were twinkling at us from the distant New Jersey shore, and Marian talked of her plans to perform the mass again, and particularly to bring it to Manhattan, in memory of Mary Lou. Before we finished, prompted by the thought that Mary Lou Williams was her first guest on *Piano Jazz*, I asked Marian whether she had any other favourites from the countless shows she'd done.

"It's hard to pick because jazz people are so individual that each show takes on the personality of the guest, and they're all so different. But I think my own personal favourite is the one I did with Bill Evans. It seems to have become very well-known, and copies have gone world-wide. I am still mad at him for dying. I couldn't believe he'd gone back on drugs at that late stage in his life because on the show he was so together, so much fun, it seemed impossible. That programme was really a high point in my career. And perhaps the other one I'd single out is Teddy Wilson. He wasn't known for being verbose, but maybe he felt safe with me, and just talked. Also, he didn't suffer fools gladly, and he told me that he liked his interviewers to be well-briefed. If it was a conversation on the phone, for example, and the interviewer clearly didn't know Teddy's music, he'd hang up. But with me, he started chatting away. I feel so good about it because in the future if people *really* want to know what Teddy Wilson was like, they can hear it on the tape of that show."

Endnote:
1. The Carlo Krahmer sides were made on a subsequent visit back to Britain in 1949. Marian's first discs were made on her 1946 visit, although the three tracks that included Jimmy have not been issued. However, she appeared with the rhythm section in a quartet with guitarist Vic Lewis that has been commercially released.

21 oscar peterson

This interview was first published in the March 2000 issue of *Piano*. Ever since I first heard Oscar Peterson in person, playing solo in Oxford's New Theatre, while I was an undergraduate in 1972, I have been in awe of his playing. Later, I contributed notes to a number of his Telarc albums, but it never quite worked out that we were able to talk face to face. We finally met when he played at a reunion of the Very Tall Band with Milt Jackson and Ray Brown at the Blue Note in New York in November 1999. The results of their music-making were issued by Telarc, forming an accurate reflection of one of the last public meetings of these three giants of jazz. The day after their opening night, Oscar kindly spent much of the afternoon with me, and this conversation was the result. I am also glad to have had the opportunity to assist in helping his autobiography *Jazz Odyssey* into print, as it gives a very thorough and rounded portrait of this truly remarkable man.

It seems incredible that in August this year [2000], Oscar Peterson will be seventy-five. In every way a giant of the piano, and having bounced back from serious illness at the start of the 1990s, Peterson still projects youthfulness and vigour in his playing. Offstage he may be slower in his movements than before, but at the piano his right hand darts across the keyboard with a speed and accuracy seldom equalled in the history of jazz piano.

Peterson's touring group, nowadays a quartet rather than the famous trio of old, is kept busy in the world's large concert halls, and Peterson himself thinks of it as his "NATO" group: an alliance between himself (a Canadian), the Swedish guitarist Ulf Wakenius, the Danish bassist Niels-Henning Ørsted-Pedersen, and the British drummer Martin Drew, whom Peterson ranks as one of the finest anywhere in the world, firmly debunking the notion that Europeans cannot match their transatlantic colleagues when it comes to jazz. The quartet's latest album, *A Summer Night In Munich*, catches the group's ability to create delicate chamber jazz even in a large auditorium such as the München Philharmonika.

Yet, for almost the first time in his busy career, Peterson is also looking back. In January [2000] he released his own selection of his best work from the 1960s and 1970s for his German producer Hans-Georg Brunner-Schwer, showing off his playing in every context from solo piano to trio, and from full orchestra to Singers Unlimited. The results are on *My Personal Choice*.

When I met him in the quiet calm of his hotel suite, a dozen floors above the busy bustle of the Manhattan streets, our conversation also began by looking back, in this case to Norman Granz's touring Jazz At The Philharmonic (JATP) concerts during the 1940s and 1950s, in which Peterson had his debut in New York, after Granz persuaded him to travel down from Canada. "You know I cherish those days because they did a lot for me in the way of development," he began. "Playing with all those wonderfully great players, Coleman Hawkins, Dizzy, Roy Eldridge, Benny Carter, Ella and so forth, was a great training ground for me, and I still appreciate what it gave me.

"One of the things I really learned from JATP was standing in the wings whenever Hank Jones played for Ella. I learned an awful lot about accompaniment from him because that was all new to me. I hadn't been playing as an accompanist at any time in my career up to that point, but I learned so much that when Hank left I eventually took over the spot. Observing him made it a lot easier for me, it really did."

I suppose I'd always thought of Peterson as such a natural accompanist, it had never occurred to me that he must have had to learn this aspect of his craft, but talking to a number of other pianists recently from Tommy Flanagan to Junior Mance, Hank Jones's importance to modern jazz piano and the art of accompaniment has been stressed by all of them. Oscar Peterson, however, garnered the added experience of having to find just the right backdrop for virtually all the high-profile soloists who appeared at Granz's concerts.

"Everybody wanted something different," he recalled. "Prez (Lester Young) wanted a simple, floating, swinging time behind him. Dizzy wanted you involved the whole time with a sock-it-to-me kind of thing, and also for almost every song he had slightly different chords he always wanted you to use, so when it got to his turn to take a solo, you had to remember 'Uh oh! Dizzy's chords!' So everyone had their own wants and wishes for accompaniment, and we, that's to say my trio with Ray Brown and Herb Ellis, plus whoever was on drums on that tour, had to satisfy that.

Oscar Peterson in 1959 (Mike Doyle/Symil)

"And there were other characteristics they all had as well. Roy Eldridge, we called him 'Speedy,' was always ready for a battle. He used to love what they called 'strollers,' which is when the piano and the guitar would lay out, and all of a sudden it was just the bass, the drums and Roy, which really changed the tone colour in his solos. Then there was the 'ballad set,' and what was beautiful about that was because it wasn't to do with picking one tune and everyone playing solos on that, but getting variety and colour into a set by everyone playing a chorus or two of a different tune. Oftentimes the trombonist Bill Harris would play *The Nearness Of You*. Coleman Hawkins might play *Body And Soul* or he might surprise us with something else. Lester Young might play *Tea For Two* at a ballad tempo, so the whole tonal colour of the set changed from artist to artist and piece to piece. They'd come on one at a time, but they weren't separated by any kind of intermission or pause. They just kept arriving one after another, so we really had to be on our toes."

Oscar's debut at JATP was recently reissued as part of *The Complete Jazz At The Philharmonic on Verve 1946–1949*. And, as we got talking about how different musicians could change the whole character of a JATP performance, I suggested to Oscar that, in a very similar way, the different bassists, drummers or guitarists who had worked in his own trio had brought about wide-ranging alterations in the way he tackled his own performances. "Yes," he agreed. "The most aggressive of all the drummers in the trio was Bobby Durham. And Ed Thigpen was the neatest. It was a kick for me because there was such an interchange of strong musical personalities in those days. I'm not so sure that it's the same today because of the kind of format in which our performances are set. You still have the vibrancy, I think, but you don't have those momentary changes you used to get as a consequence of these strong characters. But then it was always quite a thing to change one member of our group because our arrangements were so tightly knit that whoever the new man was really had to take time to get the parts together, so he was under a handicap until he felt easy."

I wondered at this point whether Oscar ever felt a prisoner of his own success in the trio, hidebound by audience expectations into playing a small number of his hit tunes, and unable to keep evolving. "We tried to keep evolving because I changed the library around. It might be a tedious task, but if you were to go through all of my LPs from those days, you'd find the repertoire and approach are quite different from one to another, even when the same people in the group were together for quite a while. The parts were fairly intricate, and, even coming back to some of the tunes we were asked to play a lot, each player gave them a different meaning. I like to think we were all open souls."

At the time we met, Oscar was briefly back together with his old sidekick Ray Brown for some club and recording dates. Ray described their relationship as "almost like a marriage," and Oscar agreed that, of the whole *mélange* of bassists with whom he had worked, Ray stood out, as did his current bassist Niels-Henning Ørsted-Pedersen. "Niels is a phenomenal player in his own right, and his knowledge of the instrument combines with a swinging proficiency, but what's really outstanding about him are his solo ideas, which are so advanced they become a catalyst within the group. They inspire us on to other ideas of our own. He's a great contrast to my other long-term bassist, the late Sam Jones. Now, Sam didn't play many solos, but he was a very directional player, he had a great sense of time, and that again brought something different to the group: a deep-rooted sound we all used to love."

Mention of Niels-Henning set Oscar off on a different tack, and suddenly we were no longer looking back, but savouring his enthusiasm for his current quartet and looking forward to the next concerts. "The thing that really intrigues me about this current group is the enthusiasm. We come off stage, and there's such great musical love for one another, we all grab each other by the hand and say 'Man, that was something else!' I might even accuse somebody of climbing up my back musically, and they'll say 'Wait 'til tomorrow night!' It's a wonderful feeling to be that effervescent about a performance.

"Perhaps part of it is an underlying agreement we have in the quartet, which goes back to a view I've always had as long as I've been playing. And that is that we owe the public. If we step up there, we owe them, and without being too squishy about it, I say to everyone in the quartet: 'If you really don't feel like playing, then don't step over that line on to the stage, we'll go and do it on our own, whoever's left.'

"I think that feeling goes back to when I was growing up in Montreal, and all the great performers were coming through town. Ellington, Basie, Nat Cole, and so on. I remember the great musical expectancy I had. We'd say 'Duke's coming!' or 'Nat's coming!' and I couldn't wait to see and hear them. And I think that sense is still there in the public that attends jazz concerts. We played a concert recently in Buenos Aires, and we played to over 30,000 people in an outdoor park, which is an unusual situation. But when the concert was over, we got mobbed. My little daughter was with me, and she was totally frightened because hordes of people were climbing all over the car, and she didn't know what was going on. For me, on the other hand, it was wonderful! I love the kind of emotion that happens when you really get through to an audience like that. Because that's the whole intent of what I do, to communicate my feelings musically."

One striking example of that communication is Oscar's work both as a teacher at York University, Toronto, and also as a mentor for young musicians, of whom the outstanding example is his "official protégé," pianist Benny Green. "The main thing I love about Benny Green is the quality of real enthusiasm he has for what he is doing," said Oscar. "You have to have that and a belief in yourself, and he has both of those things, plus he has great talent. I've always admired someone who comes into the jazz field with respect for those who've gone before. Classical players have to learn respect for the work of the great masters, and I think it should be the same in jazz because there are certain individuals that gave so much, like Ellington and Tatum, and so on down the line. If you don't study them, I think you're lacking in a grounding and a foundation. Benny's not lacking because he listens intently to these people and their work."

There could be no better example of how both mentor and protégé are aware of the tradition, but also listen intently to one another when playing together, than their joint CD *Oscar And Benny*. I wrote the liner notes for this, and needed some gentle help from both pianists in identifying exactly which of them was playing what, so closely are their styles and ideas bound up with one another, and, as we talked again about the session, Oscar laughed at the memory. "I think we were very productive at that session, and indeed I think I've been similarly productive in all my groups over the years, in whatever configuration. With Benny or the quartet, we've tried to retain the idea of playing for each other. You don't come into the picture as a vaunted soloist. You play solos, for sure, but you also play for the group. A perfect example of this is the newest arrival, Ulf Wakenius. As talented a guitarist as he is, he plays for me, he plays off me, and I play off him. That's what gives a group body, background and spirit. I've always looked for the group feeling, first with Ray Brown and Herb Ellis, then Ray and Ed Thigpen, and after that Sam Jones and Bobby Durham. We always felt that each of us was playing for the other two, and that's the main reason my music has worked so well over the years."

22 michel petrucciani

This interview with Michel Petrucciani is a good example of a snatched conversation before a concert which, when I went back to it after his death as the source for a radio obituary, turns out to have been more packed with insight than I thought at the time. So often, either as a BBC presenter or *Times* journalist, there's no more opportunity than a hasty chat backstage to collect essential background for a broadcast or a review. Our conversation took place in a dressing room at the Queen Elizabeth Hall in London on February 15, 1994, just before Michel went on stage for a solo set that I later presented on BBC Radio 3. It was published in this form in the July 2001 edition of *Piano*.

It is two and a half years since the premature death, aged just thirty-six, of the French pianist Michel Petrucciani [he died on January 5, 1999], but the recent posthumous release of his album *Conversations* and the promise of more previously unissued sessions to come, make this a timely moment to remember this diminutive virtuoso.

Petrucciani succeeded in becoming one of the world's top jazz pianists against seemingly impossible odds. He suffered from the rare bone disease *osteogenis imperfecta*, which left him with a diminutive stature, brittle bones and a whole string of constant minor ailments. When I met him in 1994 he was recovering from the effects of a broken bone in his foot, and he not only had to be carried on and off stage by his brother, but had difficulty operating his specially adapted pedals. Nevertheless, this barely affected his playing, which was always a triumph of indomitable will, intellect and remarkable physical control.

Michel grew up in the South of France, and began playing piano at the age of four, being confined indoors by his illness. It was soon apparent that he was a more than usually gifted musician, and it was the experience of first hearing Duke Ellington on record that prompted Michel to begin to play jazz seriously himself. As a teenager, his reputation grew through playing impressively with American expatriates such as the drummer Kenny Clarke, until he decided to move to the United States in 1982, aged just

Michel Petrucciani signing autographs after his interview with the author, Queen Elizabeth Hall, London, 1994 (Derek Drescher)

twenty. There he made his name by coaxing the saxophonist Charles Lloyd out of retirement, and making records with him and also with guitarist Jim Hall. Soon, plenty of other jazz stars were queuing up to work with him.

"I made a lot of drummers jealous when I started to work with Roy Haynes in 1987," he told me. "All the other drummers wanted to work with me after that because they figured, 'If the master wants to work with him, he's got to be good!' Roy went on the road with me for two months, and I remember Jack DeJohnette called me up and said 'Hey, is that true? Roy's gonna be working with you for two whole months?' And when I told him it was true he said it was unbelievable because Roy doesn't go out on the road away from his own band too much. So I asked Roy why he had agreed, and he told me he just wanted to check me out: to see what I was really about. A long time after that tour, I dropped in to hear him in Paris, and he called me up on stage, and asked me to play a composition of mine we'd recorded called *She Did It Again*. It's not an easy tune, and he hadn't played it in maybe five years, but he remembered the whole thing, every twist and turn of the arrangement. And afterwards he said he could remember just about every number he had ever played, which is incredible."

Michel's own musical memory was equally remarkable, as he proved often in his magnificent solo recitals where one piece flowed seamlessly into another, and there was a compelling mixture of new and old. (One of his last records, *Solo Live*, is a perfect example.) I asked him how he felt about playing solo piano:

"I really believe a pianist is not complete until he's capable of playing by himself. I started doing solo concerts in February 1993, when I asked my agent to cancel my trio dates for a year in order to play nothing but solo recitals. And at the end of that time I began a new project with a string quartet, but I had a wonderful time playing alone, and discovering the piano and really studying every night. I felt I was learning so much about the instrument and about communicating directly with an audience. So it was an incredible experience. I really loved doing that, and afterwards getting on stage with a group again and playing with other people was a piece of cake!"

His first solo records were made when he was just seventeen, but by the time he reached his thirties for that twelve-month solo stint, his playing had matured considerably. Yet, he told me, he still remembered the thing that drew him to the piano as a child was its very completeness as an instrument: "You can be percussive, you can be harmonic, you can be melodic, and I really love the physical aspect of playing the instrument. A long time ago, I made an allusion to the piano, saying that when I opened the keyboard it was a row of teeth, smiling up at me, but also sinister, asking 'Well, what are you gonna do with me now?' I think that was my child's imagination. Now, I want to feel that my playing is so clear that you would be able to sing every note I play. If I can achieve that, then I'm happy because it's like language – you want to go straight to the point. I think the preponderant thing in my style is that clarity in my touch. Of course the pitfall is that when I make a mistake it sounds absolutely outrageous, really horrible because everything else is so clear!"

Michel was very sure of his ideas, and that they would carry him through areas where his technique might not. As we ended our conversation together, I asked him if he was one of those people who heard music in his head all the time. His face clouded, and he said, "No. In fact music for me is becoming like a torture. It's something so serious, so intense, that I'm scared to think about it. I orchestrate my time and there's a time when I close the store – I do other things – but when the shop is open I really concentrate on music."

I was lucky enough to hear Michel several times when the shop was well and truly open, and he proved himself to be one of the most inventive and technically brilliant of all jazz pianists, until he was finally struck down by a lung infection. It is our good fortune that he recorded so much material during his short life that much of his best work is only now being issued for the first time.

23 horace silver

When Horace Silver's four-CD *Retrospective* set came out from
Blue Note in 2000, I went to interview him about it for the
BBC World Service. Once we'd done the honours for the radio
regarding the album, we settled down for a longer conversation, most of which appears here for the first time.

I think the earliest discs on which I spotted Horace's name in the line-up
are those he made with Stan Getz for Roost in the early 1950s. So when
we met at his home in California, overlooking the Pacific, I began by asking if these were, indeed, Horace's first recordings.

"Yes, they are. I met Stan in 1950, when I was working up in Hartford,
Connecticut in a club called the Sundown. It was a little black nightclub
and I had five nights a week working there with my trio. We played floor
shows for dancing every Friday and Saturday, but the other three days
we could play what we wanted. A lot of the local guys would come in
and jam, so we started having jam sessions, and after a while these settled to be on Thursday nights and became pretty popular. Before long
the owner of the club got the idea of every so often bringing in a name
person from New York to attract even more people to the jam session.
The first one he brought up was Lucky Thompson. He played with us
and liked our rhythm section, to the extent that he said that he'd like to
use us sometime. We just laughed and thought he was putting us on,
but a week afterwards we got a letter from him suggesting we do some
work together. As it turned out, that never did materialize, but about four
weeks after that they brought up Stan Getz as the guest star.

"He said exactly the same, that he liked us and would like to use us,
but once more we just laughed, thinking nothing would come of it, like
last time. Then, two weeks later he called and invited us to join him.
So the three of us, Walter Bolden on drums, Joe Calloway on bass and
myself, packed up and went. I ended up playing for him for about a year
and a half. Stan had a much lighter tone in those days, when he was a
young player. It's funny, but I noticed the same thing with Lester Young,
that in his early career he had a nice light fluffy tone, but in the years

after he left Basie, it got heavier and heavier and heavier. It was like that with Stan, in those early formative years, before his tone got darker. He told me once, much later, that it was because he used to use a particular mouthpiece, and one day it got stolen with his horn. He never found a comparable mouthpiece, and never recaptured that early tone."

Having established that Horace met Stan in Hartford, what had been the steps that got him there in the first place?

"I just lucked out on that particular job. Before that I was working weekends round my home town of Norwalk, Connecticut, and trying to make it as a musician. My mother had died when I was nine years old, so there was just me and Dad. One day he came to me and told me that the money I was making, by only playing on some weekends, and not working on others, wasn't bringing in enough to put food on the table. So he told me I was

Horace Silver in the 1960s (Redferns)

going to have to get a job in a factory. So reluctantly I did, but I didn't like it, and I resolved to get my music together because I didn't want to be doing hard manual labour for the rest of my life! After several months at the factory, the phone rang and it was my friend the drummer Walter Bolden, calling me from Hartford, to say that the pianist at the Sundown, where he was working, had just quit, and did I want the job? His mother agreed to rent me a room, and the money sounded okay, so I took it! Compared to Norwalk, which was a small town, Hartford was the state capital, and it had a whole lot going on. There were many black and white musicians there who were really into music, and who played good jazz. I remember quite a few other clubs as well as the Sundown, and of course there was the State Theater where all the big bands used to play."

So, now Horace had moved from Norwalk to Hartford, become known through his work with Stan Getz, and made his first discs. What did he do next, in what was, by then, 1951?

"I decided I wanted to stay in New York to get my local 802 union card. In order to do that you had to prove residence for six months, except you could only work one night a week. Now obviously you can't live on one gig a week, but fortunately I had put aside some money from my time with Stan, and that helped to tide me over. And luckily somebody offered me a regular gig each weekend over the river in New Jersey. Now that was outside the State of New York, but only about forty-five minutes' drive away, and it paid ten dollars a night. So with thirty dollars a week from that, playing Friday through Sunday, and what I had saved, I was just about able to survive the six months.

"When I got my card, I knocked about playing with a lotta different groups around town. Name bands, no-name bands. Floor shows. Dances."

How long had it taken before Horace wound up at the Café Bohemia?

"Oh, probably a couple of years. It was a nice club. Actor Canada Lee's son Carl Lee was the *maître d'* there. I worked there with Oscar Pettiford and The Jazz Messengers, and I always enjoyed working there."

Mention of The Messengers prompted me to ask how it was formed.

"I had done three or four trio recordings for Blue Note, and they asked me to do another one. So I said I'd like to use some horns, and Alfred Lion said 'Yeah okay.' I used Kenny Dorham, Hank Mobley, Doug Watkins, Art Blakey and myself. We rehearsed and did one ten-inch album. He liked it and then we did another, and those two included tunes like *Doodlin,' The Preacher, Room 608*. As a result of doing those two albums, we got together, the musicians that is, and said, 'Hey, we sound pretty good together, we gel. We ought to keep this going.' So that's what started the Jazz Messengers."

The trio records had come about as a result of Horace's friendship with altoist Lou Donaldson, who had introduced him to Blue Note. They had met while Horace was living in the Bronx, through a mutual friend, Arthur Woods, a great jazz fan and also an amateur musician who tried to play alto, but whose main work was in a film distribution company.

"He knew all the cats, and hung out with Bird, Bud Powell and all the guys. Arthur introduced me to Lou, following which we played on a couple of jam sessions, and we ended up becoming friends. Lou used me on a couple of his gigs, I used him on a couple of mine, and eventually I wound up playing on his first Blue Note record session with bassist Gene Ramey and drummer Art Taylor."

Donaldson's regular drummer was Art Blakey, who did not make that date, but he was booked for a planned return to the studio on October 9, 1952. For some reason, now long forgotten, Donaldson cancelled this date three days before it was due to take place, but Alfred Lion called Silver and asked him if he would take it on with Ramey and Blakey as a trio session.

"It was an opportunity, and I had plenty of tunes written because I've been writing music since I was fourteen or fifteen years old. Speaking of which, most of my music comes by telepathy. It comes to me in my sleep, and I get up and write down what I hear. I try to write melodies that'll catch on, are simple to play and simple to understand. I try to write the kind of music that, when I play a new tune, has the kind of simplicity and depth that people will go home singing, and carry with them."

He pulled his repertoire together during the customary rehearsal that Lion subsidized before the making of any Blue Note session. The numbers they cut included a piece called *Safari* that had an insistent Latin left-hand pattern comparable to Powell's *Un Poco Loco*, which gives way to one of the trademarks of Silver's playing, in which his left hand grumbles along playing repeated notes, alternating notes or repeated chords. It is a slightly muddy, but entirely original, approach to how a pianist might accompany right-hand bebop improvisations, but when I asked him how he came to develop it he had no explanation:

"My left hand thing, that's something that came to me very unconsciously. I can't tell why. I just started playing like that and it happened. It was like I had no control over my left hand, it just went crazy and took off by itself. All of a sudden. I didn't consciously programme it to do that."

I suggested to Horace that, apart from his left hand, the other most distinctive element in his compositions and playing was the sound of the black church.

"That Gospel feel? Well it's both a 'yes' and 'no' in terms of my background. I didn't go to black churches as a kid because my dad was Portuguese, so I went to Catholic school and church. But my mother was black Methodist and I would occasionally go to her church and dig the singing there. But I think the real thing that brought it into my music was that my godmother in South Norwalk lived a block away from a storefront sanctified church. Sometimes when I'd pass by, they'd be swinging, so I'd stop and listen. They'd have tambourines, drums, a sax, maybe a trombone, they'd be cooking! And I fell in love with that kind of music."

To me it appeared that this influence may be responsible, at least in part, for the way Horace, Blakey and Doug Watkins managed to simplify the sound of the bebop rhythm section. They kept its harmonic complexity but pared away at the kind of polyrhythmic approach pioneered by Max Roach, stripping it down to its bare, hard-swinging essentials. But Horace didn't see what they did as anything like so carefully planned: "We weren't trying to do nothing but just cook, swing, make it happen. We weren't consciously striving for any specific thing. We called Art 'Little Dynamo' because he had so much drive, power, swing. When you played with him you had to match up to him. You had to play strong when you played with Art Blakey. When I played with Kenny Clarke, I had to change my whole thing around because he was softer and a little more delicate. He swings just as hard, but he's not as loud. Art was loud, what you might call robust, you know? Primitive. You had to match up so as not to sound like a weakling or a fool."

When Horace first proposed to Alfred Lion that he record with a quintet, had he any idea that the quintet format would become the predominant setting in which he would be heard for the rest of his musical life?

"No, but looking back at it, it was the best alternative. Because of finances it wasn't possible to work with a big band, and we liked the smaller setting because we could all blow more. Also, a quintet was financially feasible. When we started, I think Kenny Dorham and Hank Mobley were great musicians who were somewhat under-rated. Doug Watkins, too. He was a great timekeeper, with fantastic swing. In fact, I liked all their musicianship."

Had Horace had a similarly close relationship with Alfred Lion as he had to the other musicians in the band?

"He was great to work with. Just about everything I learned about making a record, I learned from Alfred Lion. I would observe what he was doing, and he let me get involved in things other than playing. I would write the music, arrange the music, rehearse the music, record the music, and he would join me to listen to the playbacks and I'd take part in all the editing and mixing. I wanted to be involved in all the other elements of the record business, too. Other guys did the session and that was it. I'd want to know about the photo that was going on the cover. I didn't want one that I didn't like personally. 'Who's going to write the notes? Will you let me see them before you print them?' I got involved in all of that. I stayed there for so many years because he let me do my thing musically, didn't interfere in the choice of musicians or tunes, but he always involved me in so much more of the business."

Had Frank Wolff, Alfred's partner in Blue Note, made a similar impression?

"One thing I remember about Frank was that we would all go out to eat a lot. Alfred knew all the great restaurants round New York, and maybe one week we'd go to an Italian place, then a week later we'd go to a German, or a Greek or a French restaurant. But the more Alfred and I got into ordering the different specialities of these various places, Frank would always order the same thing – lamb chops. He was the lamb chop cat!

"But the two of them had a very close partnership; they discussed the music and cared about it, but at the same time they left the musical decisions up to me. That's why I stayed with them for so long. I suppose when my various contracts expired, I could have gone some place else for a few more dollars, but I decided to stay because they never insisted on which musicians I should use, or what tunes I should put on a record."

During his early Blue Note years, Horace recorded with Miles Davis (also appearing on a number of Miles's Prestige sessions). The memory is vivid. "Those discs were the first time I'd even met Miles, let alone played with him. He was on drugs in those days and I don't think he even had a horn for a while because I think he'd pawned it. Alfred loved the way Miles played, and he got him a horn from somewhere, and set up the session. Now Miles could play his butt off, but because he hadn't been playing regularly he had no chops. He was weak, and hadn't been practising, so he played at the most on one or maybe two takes of every song because if he blew any more, he'd get weak, and wouldn't be able to play any longer. But when he played, it was amazing because practice or no practice he played so brilliantly. I don't think we had the usual Blue Note rehearsal before that session either."

So, in addition to recording with his own groups and making this session for Miles, who else had Horace been working with in the early 1950s?

"I played with Oscar Pettiford at a place called Snookie's, I played with Terry Gibbs, and with Flip Phillips's trio, in which the third member was J. C. Heard on drums. I did a few gigs with J. J. Johnson, and made a few records with Milt Jackson, although I never did any gigs with him. I also recorded with Art Farmer and Gigi Gryce, and then I played with Coleman Hawkins and Lester Young.

"Lester was the most unique man I ever met in my life, with the possible exception of Thelonious Monk, who was also a remarkable individual. Pres [Lester's nickname] not only played differently, but he talked differently, and he invented a lot of the musicians' slang that we still use today. Back then if you didn't understand him when he was talking in his own way, using his own individual language, well, tough! When I'm round the musicians I talk slang, but when I'm mixing with ordinary people, lay people, I talk the normal, regular way. But not Lester! He talked one way, his way, and if you didn't understand him, you were in trouble. He dressed different as well.

"His manager Charlie Carpenter called me up one day and said Pres wanted me to join him, and our first gig was at Minton's Playhouse. We went in there for a week. There was no rehearsal, we just went in there and played. Then we went to Boston, then some dances in Michigan. I was only with him for a month or two, but it was a memorable time. Pres had a marvellous sense of humour, but at the same time he was a very introverted individual. For example, he didn't mingle with the audience after a set; he went right back to the dressing room and stayed there until the next set, drinking his little Scotch. But he kept all of us in the band in stitches, telling jokes and stories. If we didn't laugh at the stories themselves, his lingo kept us laughing because it was so strange."

Having mentioned Monk, and given that Horace had often recorded his own interpretations of pieces from Monk's repertoire, despite the fact that they were written in such an individual way, how did Horace approach Monk's music?

"Well, I love his pieces, although I should say that my first love from that period was Bud Powell. I was a teenager when I first encountered Monk's music. It was while I was still in high school and I was living in Norwalk, but I used to go down to Stamford on weekends to take this girl out. She was a little older than I, and after seeing a movie or something we'd go to her place and listen to records. She had some Monk records, and that was when I first heard him, and my initial reaction was that he was fooling everybody, and that he couldn't be serious. So I didn't pay too much attention, but as the weekends went past I listened more and more to her collection of his records, and began to realize what he was doing. I finally met him a few years later through Art Blakey, and used to go to his house sometimes, listen to him play and hang out.

"One time I was at the Baroness Nica de Koenigswater's place, her hotel suite in Manhattan, with bassist Doug Watkins, and I was playing something on her piano. The doorbell rang, and in came Monk. He stood over me listening and looking. Suddenly he leaned over, put his hands on the keys and said, 'Hey! That part there. Why don't you play it like this?' Then he proceeded to play it as he would.

"I said, 'Okay, but I think I prefer it the way I played it.'

"He paused, looked at me hard, and said, 'You're just afraid people will say you're trying to sound like me if you play it the way I showed you!' I didn't respond to that at the time, but I realized that if I was going to play his music I was going to do it my way."

To round off our discussion, we looked again at the *Retrospective* set, and I asked Horace about his various quintet line-ups down the years. He told me how Art Farmer would double between his band and Gerry Mulligan's, and how Donald Byrd worked with him during those weeks when Art was busy with Mulligan, as the baritonist paid more money than Horace could afford at the time. This inconsistency of front-line caused some jealousy between Bob Weinstock at Prestige and Alfred Lion at Blue Note, about poaching one another's musicians, particularly once Prestige had signed Farmer as its exclusive artist. At that point Lion was obliged to hire Byrd for Horace's discs, even though Farmer was still working on some of the live gigs.

"It's too bad that I didn't get to record with Art more often than I did. Another quintet I'd like to have recorded more was a few years later, during the time when both Brecker Brothers were with me. Alfred had sold Blue Note to Liberty, and its new owners were trying to negotiate a new contract with me. The result was that, for much of the time Randy and Michael were in the band, I was without a contract. They did record with me, but on our live concerts it was a hell of a band, with Alvin Queen on drums plus Will Lee on Fender bass, and the discs don't capture the extent to which it was a cooking band. Of course Randy had played and recorded with me earlier with Billy Cobham and Benny Maupin, which was another wonderful line-up. Billy Cobham used to look like he was having a ball, laughing and grinning all the time, the way Billy Higgins used to. When he got up there, started smiling, and got to swinging, I'd look over from the piano and think, 'He's having such a good time, I want to get in on some of this as well!'

"But maybe my favourite front-line of all was Blue Mitchell and Junior Cook. Blue Mitchell had played in several rhythm and blues bands before he came to New York, and soon after Lou Donaldson introduced us, I hired him as the permanent replacement for Art Farmer. He was very warm and lyrical, and as a team with Junior they could play very well round the entire repertoire. If you were doing something funky, they could get down in the pocket and play funky. If you were doing the bebop thing, they did that brilliantly. If you played Latin, they played Latin, and it was the same with a ballad or a blues as well. They could get into all these contexts and play well, and I think that it was that versatility that made them so special for me."

24 esbjörn svensson

These two interviews came three years apart. The first appeared in the May 2001 issue of *Piano*, shortly after Esbjörn Svensson's inaugural visit to Britain. The second was published in *Jazzwise*, and dates from 2004, by which time his trio had won the BBC International Artists of the Year award. I have had the opportunity to hear the trio several times, and have been equally impressed on each occasion at their sense of ensemble, the degree of interactivity between the members, and their steady progress towards achieving a highly individual sound.

Something unusual is going on in Sweden. I can't think of another country in the world where a straightforward acoustic jazz trio would see their latest album immediately jump to number fifteen in the pop charts, nor have the accompanying video played on MTV. But that's exactly what's happened to the piano, bass and drums line-up led by Swedish pianist Esbjörn Svensson, and known locally as EST (the Esbjörn Svensson Trio).

I first became aware of the band when I started to get requests from various parts of Europe on my weekly BBC World Service radio programme for its last-but-two album, *From Gagarin's Point Of View*, and particularly for a brilliantly original track that mixed a languorous free-form ballad with gritty passages of hard-hitting funk, called *Dodge The Dodo*. At that point I hadn't even heard the group, but I quickly became a convert, and sought out their next album *Winter In Venice*. Here again was the same mixture of originality and the jazz tradition, the feeling of a band that could make things happen in live performance and somehow transfer a sense of excitement to disc. All three of the band, bassist Dan Berglund, drummer Magnus Öström and Svensson himself play a variety of percussion, and, in their live sets, which tend to be an hour's music shifting seamlessly from one piece to the next, there are plenty of opportunities to add percussive shadings to whichever of the trio is taking the lead.

The title track of their new [2001] album, *Good Morning Susie Soho*, has its roots in their first extended stay in Britain, when they played a season at the Pizza Express in Soho.

"I wrote the tune while we were at the club for a few days in February last year," said Svensson. "I didn't have a title for it, and after we'd finished our run, on the last morning before we caught the plane back to Sweden, Dan and Magnus took me to a café not far from Dean Street, and it felt just like the first day of spring. We sat outside having a great cup of coffee and a chat, and Magnus, who always thinks of our titles, suddenly came up with the name."

The album has one or two effects that don't fit with the band's impressive live act. For a start, there are a few passages of overdubbing, where Svensson adds additional keyboards, but some of the things I thought were the products of the studio are integral to the way they normally play.

"Live is live," said Esbjörn, "and the basic sound of this group is all about live performance. But Dan has a few unusual things he does on the albums which you do hear us play live. For example, he uses the bow a lot, and he also plays through an effects unit with a wa-wa pedal. Not many acoustic bassists do that, but it brings a different voice into his solos, that all of us really like a lot. We are really interested in contrasts, between different types of sound, and between different feelings. So in a piece like *Dodge The Dodo*, to be able to hear what's going on in those fast sections, to pick out the action from the chaos, you need some passages of calm, otherwise you won't be hungry to hear the more challenging sections. To me, a lot of what we do is about contrast."

I pointed out that the new album is very largely about contrast, between stately dance-like compositions such as his *Pavane* or the heady rush of a piece called *Providence*, that takes off with the kind of nail-biting excitement in which the listener is constantly wondering if the band can possibly sustain this level of invention much longer. When it finally comes to an end, the record company has left in the shrieks and whoops of delight from the musicians.

"Yes, that was unusual," said Esbjörn. "I think that was the first take. We just went into the studio and played, and the way it came out was so funny we just ended up crying and laughing."

So, when most musicians in their twenties are trying to get into the charts with a rather different kind of music from jazz, what led him to set up a piano trio?

"This trio began in 1993. Magnus and I had played together for a long time, but when Dan joined was in April or May of '93, and that's when we began touring and recording. In England I think only three or four of our discs have been released, but back in Sweden there are now six, and even though the first ones were for tiny labels, I'm sure it's helped. I think we got into the charts in Sweden because of our music. I mean, I

Esbjörn Svensson at the Cheltenham Jazz Festival, 2001 (Derek Drescher)

don't think it's because we're particularly cute, and we don't think much about our image in the way pop bands do. Of course, when the music is done and recorded, we try to operate in a very commercial way; we think about the packaging, the photos, but ultimately I think it's because a lot of young people really like our live music very, very much.

"It's funny because, when I was at school, Magnus and I had our very first trio, with an electric bass player, and I sang as well, trying to play rock and roll, a bit like Jerry Lee Lewis. But that was when I began the concept of a piano-bass-drums trio, and I guess Magnus and I had our first jazz trio not long after that when we were still just seventeen years old. I think whatever drew us to do that strikes the same chord in today's young audience. There's a lot of bad things on TV or radio, and they come to hear us at one of our gigs, and they get caught up in the mood, in the spirit of the moment."

> Three years on, we met again on London's South Bank. For this interview, Esbjörn and I were joined by Dan and Magnus. I decided to try and write a piece that caught something of the group dynamics between them.

From the moment I first heard the band on its first British visit during the Swedish Jazz Extravaganza in 1999, it was obvious that the Esbjörn Svensson Trio – now known just by its initials EST – was something out of the ordinary. Playing the standard repertoire, it has incredible depth and lyricism, delving deep into the works of Thelonious Monk, for example, and finding plenty of new things to say. But alongside that is a startling new repertoire, mainly written by Svensson himself, that takes the trio into abstraction, into hard-edged drum 'n' bass grooves from drummer Magnus Öström, into Hendrix-like distortions by bassist Dan Berglund, and also into a string of memorable original melodies that keep popping into the mind for days after hearing them.

When the group appeared last year [2003] at Birmingham's CBSO Centre, Esbjörn asked the audience what they wanted the trio to play, and it was an unusual experience to hear the capacity crowd yelling out relatively obscure titles from the band's string of albums, *Winter In Venice*, *From Gagarin's Point Of View*, *Good Morning Susie Soho* and *Strange Place For Snow*. These might not seem to be mainstream listening exactly, but those in the know make every effort to hear the trio live. In return, the trio has worked hard at building up a loyal public here in Britain, as well as in most of the other territories in which it plays. It's a live act that's unpredictable, invariably different, with a structure that changes from night to night and venue to venue. As well as featuring Esbjörn's highly distinctive touch on the piano, it includes a subtle range of keyboard effects, a rather less subtle range of bass effects, and Magnus's incredible expressive range as a drummer. The band also knows how to build excitement out of nowhere, starting gently and ending up unleashing mayhem, the musicians' collective radar somehow indicating exactly what to do, and when, so that they appear to think and breathe together.

The gritty, clubby set, full of funk grooves and plangent tones that they turned out for the teen-to-twenty-something crowd in the Miles Davis Hall during last year's Montreux Festival could hardly have been more different from the dreamily reflective quality of their show at this year's Cheltenham Festival, which was admirably suited to their – how shall I put this? – more mature audience. Appearing in the United States they were favourably compared to Brad Mehldau's current trio, and, having just finished a coast-to-coast tour supporting k. d. lang, they're well advanced on the long haul into achieving the kind of recognition Stateside that they have painstakingly built up in Europe.

Their European profile itself has just taken a further upward turn when the trio became International Artists of the Year at the BBC Jazz Awards, an event neatly timed to precede the release in July 2004 of their latest album *Seven Days Of Falling*. And it's with that album that we began our conversation backstage at the QEH (Queen Elizabeth Hall) on the day of the BBC ceremony. Is it a consolidation of what they've achieved so far, or more about looking to the future?

Esbjörn: That's hard to judge. We never really know where we are...

Dan: ...or where we're going.

Esbjörn: The next step might be in another direction, but this is the step we took.

Alyn: In the past there have been stories behind the titles of your tunes and albums – what's behind the name *Seven Days Of Falling*?

Magnus: It might be different things for each of us.

Esbjörn: That's true – but to fall is what we do every time we go up on stage. We try to fall, let go of control, to fall in love with the music, let everything else fall away and immerse ourselves in the sound. There may be other meanings, but that's what it is for me.

Magnus: That's the kind of idea I had when I came up with the title – to enter free-fall, to abandon control. But it's not just about music. It might be about a relationship, to fall in love with another person...

Dan: ...or fall out of love, when you divorce, or whatever.

Alyn: There's a tension in the album between some of the pieces – like the title song itself – which clearly have that feeling of falling into reflection or introspection, and others that are more frenetic. Did you set out with that kind of plan in mind?

Esbjörn: We didn't plan the album until we actually put it together, but, as always, when we were in the studio to record, we put down more stuff than you eventually hear on the disc. We tried to see each tune as a chapter in a book, and our challenge was to create a whole book. Music is so abstract you can make up this book in many different ways, but we wanted to create an abstract story that runs right through the whole album. So we spent a lot of time looking for the right sequence for that story, switching the songs around and asking each other "What do you think?" Finally we had to make some decisions, and at last we agreed that we had the right sequence.

Alyn: How do the songs evolve? Whenever I've heard you, you've mainly selected your programmes from the latest album, with occasional numbers from earlier in your work. Do you ever try out new pieces in live concerts before you get to the studio?

Dan:	We'd never performed any of these ones before we recorded them.
Magnus:	Not live, anyway, though I think we might have tried out a few things among ourselves. Earlier in the life of the group, though, we did introduce new pieces on the road, before we recorded them, but not now. These latest pieces weren't ready until shortly before we were due to record them, but even if they had been finished earlier I think we've now come to believe that it's not a good idea to play them too much before we go into the studio. That keeps them fresh.
Alyn:	Some of them aren't exactly easy – you've got some complex ideas floating around. Does recording them fix them into a form that becomes a reference for the future?
Esbjörn:	No, it's not that we need to record them to be able to play them on stage; simply rehearsing them is enough, although of course after recording you hear them a particular way. But creating a reference or documenting isn't what we're trying to do. We're aiming to make an album, and we're lucky if we catch the best moment for a particular tune on that particular day. The minute we start playing the pieces live...
Dan:	...we're going to change them.
Esbjörn:	Actually they change themselves while we are playing them.
Alyn:	Yet they stay recognizable, as you proved to your audiences here on the last tour. And you seem to have worked hard to consolidate that audience here.
Magnus:	It's been great from the very first gig at Pizza Express, although I think the first time we played there the audience was largely Swedish people who were in town for the Extravaganza. But when we came back the next time it started to build up, and then the time after that, in addition to playing the club we began touring and all that stuff. Before we came to the Pizza that first time, we felt it was going to be really tough to get into the UK market.
Esbjörn:	The tour we did last October [2003] was a big success – especially outside London – and everywhere we were playing to big audiences.
Alyn:	Knowledgeable ones, too?
Esbjörn:	That was unbelievable. It was fun that they knew our music, and it made us very happy.
Alyn:	On that tour you were travelling with your own sound and lighting engineers, who seemed to share your instinctive feel

Esbjörn:	for the music. Are they both a permanent feature now? And what do you do about the lights when you play a club date?
Esbjörn:	We don't use the lights in clubs. We only bring Kristoffer Berg, our lighting guy, when we can afford it, which generally means larger venues, and also ones where there is equipment already installed to work with. We don't travel with our own lighting gear, so this influences where we play on any of our tours.
Alyn:	Is Kristoffer improvising in the same way you are with the music?
Magnus:	He is. We never decide anything about the songs, or the order. So it's the same for him as for everyone in the group.
Esbjörn:	I remember the first time we played here in the QEH with Kristoffer, when some of the backstage people asked him for the song list. He said, "You go down to the bandroom and get one!" Because of course he knew there wasn't one. But everyone thinks the minute you work with lighting that there must be an elaborate plan, to use the effects in a specific way.
Alyn:	So that means the same must be true of Åke Linton, your sound engineer. You credit him as the "fourth member of the trio" on your concerts, and he must share some of the same intuition that you three have in your playing to know exactly what will happen next, and how to adjust the sound for the various spaces you play in.
Esbjörn:	Every room needs a specific way of playing music, and we have to find that way together.
Magnus:	It's fun when it changes. You play a church on the one hand and maybe a rock club on the other, and they're totally different. Perhaps that's particularly the case with the drums, but I like playing in really different acoustics.
Esbjörn:	It's true also for bass and piano. In a room with lots of natural reverb, it doesn't work if you play your phrases too fast. They just disappear. So for that place you'll tend to create more space in your playing, and use fewer notes. But that's another way of keeping the music fresh.
Alyn:	What about the integration of effects, from keyboards to the wa-wa bass – are there places where you don't use them, or are they so integral to the structure of some pieces that you use them anyway?
Dan:	I have to think hard, and sometimes I have to try them out in the space. But then I usually work these things out when we

	rehearse, or when we are recording a piece for the first time, so that I know how to react to different settings.
Esbjörn:	We help you to think – and we sometimes say, "No! Try that sound..." or "No, I need more of this..."
Alyn:	Another thing about your playing, Dan, is that some pieces are a real physical challenge, especially the ones with a repetitive bass figure running all the way through them, like *When God Created The Coffee Break.*
Dan:	It is a challenge, yes. It's very hard to do physically. But I like to do it, and there are a couple of similar pieces on this disc.
Magnus:	I think you are getting stronger at it – next time there'll be five pieces!
Esbjörn:	In fact the basic phrase I wrote in *Coffee Break* was really very hard for the double bass because I began it with a G-flat, I think.
Dan:	Starting on the low E-string. Which is the hardest position to begin a long phrase like that and keep it even.
Esbjörn:	But actually that rather baroque figure wasn't originally written for bass. I wrote it for the piano, and I was working on another completely different bass line. Then you started to play my line...you stole it! So it's your own fault.
Alyn:	On the various occasions I've heard that piece, there's amazing fluidity between the two of you, probably because you share that line, rather than playing different basslines. So while Dan keeps it moving Esbjörn can leave it for a while, and then he keeps it going during the bass solo...
Esbjörn:	That's back to "falling" again. We just let go, and fall together, which means we have to depend on each other.
Alyn:	Looking ahead, then, in terms of your collective direction, is America the next big challenge?
Esbjörn:	I think the next big challenge is our next concert. We have other people working with us who can worry about our careers, where we're going and so on. That allows us to care about the music, and that's the most important thing for us. It's our job, and we can't care more about playing in one place and less about playing in another. Consistency is really important, and so is to have fun with the music.
Alyn:	For all I know you might be fed up to the back teeth with each other, but the impression you give on stage – and here in the dressing room – is that it's still fun.

Esbjörn:	We really do have a lot of fun, that's true.
Dan and	
Magnus:	Yeah, we do.
Esbjörn:	But of course it's tough being together so much. We have our ups and downs, but on balance it's OK.
Magnus:	We don't socialize together so much nowadays because in our work we see more of each other than we do of our wives.
Alyn:	When you are on the road and thrown on each other's company, do you spend much time taking notice of what other piano-bass-drums trios are doing at the cutting edge, bands like Brad Mehldau's, the Bad Plus, the Necks? Or do you live in a hermetically sealed EST world of your own?
Esbjörn:	When I hear something, usually by coincidence, that I like, I check it out. But I don't go round taking notes. The first time I heard about Brad Mehldau, I got a cassette of his playing from my father. I listened to it and just fell in love with his music. So then I made an effort to check out the band. But I don't spend my time going to the store and asking, "Hey, do you have some new piano trios I ought to hear?"
Magnus:	We travel too much by plane to listen to anything much collectively.
Esbjörn:	Yes, but when we were in the States and Canada we were on the bus, and you, Magnus, asked if you could play some music, I think it may have been some country stuff – so it does still happen occasionally. But going back to Brad, it links up to a time when I was much younger and I was really trying to educate myself. I'm still trying to educate myself, listening to mainly classical stuff such as Johann Sebastian Bach or Karl Orff, but back then I was listening to Teddy Wilson, Art Tatum, Wynton Kelly, McCoy Tyner, Bill Evans, Monk, Keith Jarrett, Chick Corea, Lyle Mays – the list goes on – and although I didn't exactly check out everything they did note for note, I was listening to their atmosphere, their colour. And I was trying to find ways of playing in the same mood that they were.
Alyn:	It's funny you should single out country music and classical music because there's one track on the new album *Believe, Beleft, Below*, that uses chording and harmonies drawn from country, but with a classical feel too.
Magnus:	Don't you think there's a gospel feel as well?
Esbjörn:	Not too much. I guess that tune has a hint of gospel, but you're right, Alyn, it's more inspired by country. And prob-

ably directly inspired by things Magnus played to me. I don't have to hear much, maybe just five minutes of something, and that's enough for me to keep it inside and remember when I'm writing. The bridge is more classical – it's hard to analyse.

Magnus: Maybe there's more of a gospel feel in the rhythm, and harmonically it's closer to country.

Alyn: How new is your music? Are you one of those writers who puts things away in a drawer and then gets them out to work on years later?

Esbjörn: The music on this album is quite new. I started to work on some of the pieces last fall while we were still touring a lot, and I didn't really get to finish them, pull them together, until January or February. We recorded them in March, so they were all recorded soon after I wrote them. But I do have some things I have put to one side, and occasionally I think of one of those tunes and wonder if it's time to try it out.

Alyn: Do you still do the bulk of the writing for the band?

Esbjörn: Yes, but then we continue the work together.

Alyn: I know in the past, Esbjörn, you've had a separate musical life outside the trio, for example in your long-term collaboration with Nils Landgren, playing funk. Has the success of the trio more or less put an end to this, as well as the other independent projects that Magnus and Dan have been part of?

Dan: We have no time now for other projects.

Esbjörn: Nor even for our families!

Alyn: Do you look back to those other projects rather wistfully?

Magnus: It's always good to play with different people to get new input, but right now we're playing so much with the trio that we are all three really focused just on that. But that's also good – to have the opportunity to focus so intensely. In the longer term I think it's good for the music, good for the trio, for us to find the time occasionally to play with other musicians.

Esbjörn: Other inputs are good.

Magnus: But then we each represent a different kind of input to the trio itself, which is one of the reasons we have such a variety of music in what we play.

Esbjörn: And it's very important to take this opportunity to do everything we can with the trio. People used to talk to us about "the chance of a lifetime," but actually that's exactly what we have right now with the trio. The success we have at the moment is fantastic, and although all of us had rock bands and other

	groups while we were young, and we thought that was the way to become successful, it's ended up coming by this route instead, so let's keep on going!
Alyn:	And it's not as if you haven't been working at it for a while because, Esbjörn, weren't you at school with Magnus?
Magnus:	We grew up together, living across the street, from the age of three.
Esbjörn:	Yeah, even though we don't socialize too much now, we have a good relationship. I know all the signs when Magnus is really angry with me, or something, and we know how to deal with that.
Alyn:	I guess that helps the music, having things you don't have to explain because you know each other so well.
Esbjörn:	It's funny because we do lots of interviews where people ask us this kind of question, and to be honest they never really occur to us. We listen and think, "Oh, that's how he or she sees it!" And then there's analysis of what we play and so on, but we don't really talk to each other about what we're doing. We play rather than analyse. Then people come and tell us what they make of it, and it's really nice to hear.
Alyn:	But now and on previous occasions when we've talked, you've always been full of ideas – of stories about where and how tunes arose, or making a point like your earlier one about the "abstract story" of the present disc. So it's a bit disingenuous to suggest you don't ever analyse what you do. If I put you on the spot and asked which elements of the abstract story are most important, would you turn it on its head and say, "No, that's for you to find out"? Did you have a clear vision of that story? For example, there seems to be a link between the piano solo called *Evening In Atlantis* and the piece that follows it.
Esbjörn:	That's called *Did They Ever Tell Cousteau?* And it was the tune that we recorded first. In fact we'd made the whole album, mixed it, sequenced it and everything, and then we just had a feeling that we needed a link here, a song that would take the mood down from *Mingle In The Mincing Machine*, which was a very rhythmical piece that preceded *Cousteau* in the order. We originally recorded something else to fill the gap, but it wasn't quite right, and we knew we needed something that was not rhythmic, more impressionist. I even brought in the sheet music of a Debussy prelude to see if it might work,

but it didn't and I just improvised something. Debussy may have been in my mind, but I was more thinking about what EST needed right now. And we ended up with a typical EST contrast, going from a kind of drum 'n' bass rhythm and then going into something more relaxed. In the past, we've had contrasts within a piece, like *Dodge The Dodo*, which we play almost every night, and which has changed over time. When I wrote it, there was the bass solo, and when it finished with a kind of "boom," then the contrast appeared. Now that's gone, somebody took it away, and now there's no "boom," and the next section's floating around a bit now.

Dan: Someone changed the piano solo – that's got a bit longer...

Esbjörn: ...not to mention the ending part. It's changing from night to night, and that keeps the music alive. It's another kind of abstract story.

25 billy taylor

My first contact with Dr Billy Taylor was when I was researching my biography of Dizzy Gillespie, *Groovin' High*. Billy was
extremely helpful in building up an accurate picture of events
on 52nd Street in 1943–44 when Dizzy had the first bebop
quintet ever to have played on "the street." This was important because Dizzy was actually a year too late in the dates he
suggested for this in his own autobiography, and with Billy's
guidance I was able to locate press reports and photographs
that allowed me to reconstruct what actually happened. Consequently, when we met during a visit to the UK in which Billy
played at the Stables, Wavendon, and later at the Wigmore Hall
in London, our conversation began with a look back to that same
period on 52nd Street. It has not previously been published.

"In December 1943 I was working with Ben Webster across the street at
the Three Deuces, when Dizzy opened at the Onyx," recalled Billy Taylor,
in relaxed form at Cleo Laine and John Dankworth's kitchen table, after
rehearsing at the nearby Stables theatre. Sitting back in his chair, he went
on, "Bud Powell was supposed to be his piano player, but for a variety of
reasons he couldn't make it. The main one was that, at only nineteen, he
was under age and still under the guardianship of Cootie Williams. So,
Dizzy actually opened without a piano player, but the rest of the band
was Oscar Pettiford, Max Roach, Don Byas and himself.

"I rushed over because I wanted to learn some of the tunes they were
playing. I sat in, and Dizzy showed me the chords. He was a great teacher
and a good pianist himself, and he knew exactly what he wanted. Instead
of writing things out, he would show you how to play the particular voicings he was hearing. As a result, on that particular job I learned many of
the bebop tunes I know now.

"Ben was fine about it, until I eventually kept being so late getting back
to my real gig that I got fired! Later on, I worked together with Ben again
on many occasions, and there were no hard feelings. He was always one
of my favourite saxophone players, and because he, too, was a pianist, he

Dr Billy Taylor, London, July 1998 (Redferns)

encouraged me to do a style of comping that only a few guys were doing in those days. That really helped set my style for accompanying singers and instrumental soloists."

Looking at Billy's impressive discography, it seemed that in the fullness of time, accompanying became something of a speciality for him, not least because after leading his own trio at the Downbeat, he became the house pianist at Birdland, playing for just about everybody.

"That's right," he laughed. "As the house pianist, whenever anyone came through, I'd play for them. And funnily enough, soon after I started there, I wound up playing for Dizzy again, despite the fact that he was leading his own complete band at the club. This was because for some time in the early 1950s his line-up had himself and Milt Jackson doubling on piano, but no actual resident pianist in the band. Whenever they came to Birdland, Milt was like a brother! He'd welcome me with open arms, get up from the piano stool and focus on just playing the vibraphone. It was a wonderful band to play with. Bill Graham was the saxophonist, and as well as being a fine player he and Dizzy had comparable senses of humour, which meant you could hardly play half the time because of the antics these guys got up to."

Jumping back in time from Birdland to soon after his time at the Onyx with Dizzy, Billy had made his first trio discs in 1944 with some of the great names in the swing era, bassist Al Hall and the legendary drummer Jimmy Crawford, but he pointed out that in terms of collective skill, his first band with Ben Webster was even better.

"That rhythm section of Ben's was one of the finest I've ever played with. There was Charlie Drayton, not a great soloist, but a marvellous accompanist, who played a great section part on bass, and the drummer was Big Sid Catlett. There was no way you could sound bad with those two guys in the rhythm team. Sid had moved on by the time I came to make my own first records, but his place in Ben's band had been taken by Jimmy Crawford, and Jimmy was nice enough to work on them with me."

Those first discs were made for Savoy, but within a few years the catalogue that seemed to feature Billy the most was Prestige.

"True," grinned Billy. "I think I was the first pianist Bob Weinstock used after Lennie Tristano. Lennie was the first, but after that Bob heard some of my trios and as a result he recorded me a lot. The sound that Prestige got on piano for Red Garland, and even for Monk when he recorded for them, was to a large extent based on the way I sounded because their engineer, Rudy Van Gelder, and I worked a lot together. I had particular things I wanted to hear in the way the piano was recorded, and I didn't want to sound like Lennie Tristano, who had a different concept of how he should be heard. So Rudy and I worked to achieve what you might call the 'Prestige piano sound' on the instrument he had in his living room in Hackensack, New Jersey, where the recordings were made."

One of the musicians that Billy worked with around this time was the bassist Earl May, someone much talked about among players of Billy's generation. What was special about him?

"It was that he was different," said Billy. "I met Earl on a gig with Lester Young, and the fascinating thing about him was that he played backwards because he was left-handed. He used a conventional bass that was strung for a right-handed player, which meant that his strength in his left hand was all directed to the lower strings. He played the E and A strings with a lot more power than a normal player, where they're right up against the stomach. With him, they were further away, and he could really use them, so the result was that his sound was focused right at the bottom of the bass, and this depth gave a very special character to his playing.

"Actually for a while in the early 1950s I had another left-handed player in my trio as well, Charlie Smith, who's the drummer best known for the one surviving piece of film with Charlie Parker and Dizzy together, playing *Hot House*. You can see in that clip how he uses his left hand. So I had these two left-handed players in my group at the same time! But Charlie ought to be famous for another reason than that little piece of film. He invented a way of representing the conga drum on his kit, which is something just about all drummers use nowadays. When he was with my trio, we made a record called *Cu-Blue*. Actually Charlie wasn't on the record because Jo Jones did the session, along with a conga drummer called Frankie Colon. However, although Charlie didn't play on the date, he was a regular member of the trio at the time. When the record came out, people began requesting this number, but I would never play it because it didn't seem to have that Cuban feel without the conga drum. After a while Charlie said we could play it because he'd figured out what to do, and he took the mallet and tom toms to create this conga effect alongside the sound of the regular kit. That's why he started to do it, and from then on, as I said, many other drummers have taken it up."

Having got onto the subject of less well-known players, I asked Billy about another drummer, Buford Oliver, a one-time member of Cab Calloway's band, whom Danny Barker had discussed with me, and with whom I knew Billy had recorded.

"Actually we came to Europe together in the late forties," he recalled. "We were both with Don Redman's band, in an incredible line-up that also included Don Byas, Tyree Glenn and Peanuts Holland. I had never played with Buford before, but he was a really fine drummer who came from Detroit, and we made a couple of trio sides during that trip to France. He never really got the kind of attention he deserved."

Our conversation strayed on to one or two other lesser-known players, before we got onto the subject of how Billy's own interest in the piano developed.

"It began with my uncle. In fact all the family on my father's side were musicians. My grandfather was a Baptist minister, so we sang in church. My father played brass instruments and all his brothers and sisters played something. As there were seven of them, that's quite a collection of musicians! But I had this one uncle who sounded a bit different from all my other musical relatives. I didn't immediately identify it as jazz, although what he was playing was stride piano. I thought in those days that he sounded a bit like Fats Waller, but as my own knowledge of jazz grew I realized he was more like Willie "The Lion" Smith. I don't know if he ever knew the Lion, but that was the style that he played. He actually sounded much heavier than Waller because, for example, instead of using a single note in the right hand, he'd often use an octave, so it almost sounded like two guys playing, one down in the bass, and the other up in the treble. I really liked that, and tried to get him to teach me. But he wouldn't, and so my father sent me to have the usual piano lessons, but they didn't get me where I wanted to go. So, I went back to my uncle and said, 'Look, Uncle Bob, you've got to help!'

"Again, he said no, but he told me to go and listen to a record, which turned out to be my first Fats Waller record. I listened to that, and then to others like it, until when I pestered Uncle Bob again about teaching me, he gave me an Art Tatum record, and that got me off his back for ever!"

Although Billy's roots were in stride, he seemed to me to straddle all the styles of jazz piano.

"I certainly like all the styles, and I was fortunate enough to have Tatum as a mentor. The one thing I learned from him was to be eclectic in my listening. Art heard just about every kind of piano player you can think of, and incorporated just about everything he heard into his work. If you analyse his playing closely, in virtually any piece you hear boogie-woogie, European classical music, stride, you name it. In fact in one record, *Get Happy*, which he made for Decca in the late thirties, you hear him playing through almost all the styles that were then current, as well as pointing forward to Billy Kyle and Bud Powell and all those who followed him. All that in a single three-minute record!"

It is this ability to form a neat encapsulation of a point, learned but unstuffy, knowledgeable but informative, and easily illustrated by a recording, that has made Billy not only a great educator but a master of jazz broadcasting, and as we share the job of talking into a microphone about jazz from time to time, my last question was about how he'd got into radio and television.

"I backed into it," he laughed. "I used to do lots of interviews, and I became friendly with a number of presenters who loved jazz and wanted to know more. They tried to make a separation on the air between their work and that of those broadcasters who wouldn't let a jazz musician talk, but simply asked long involved questions that could only be followed by a yes or no. The people I met liked jazz, wanted to know more, and were prepared to listen to the answers. And so I learned about the difference between that kind of intelligent questioning, and what so often passes for jazz broadcasting. I decided to follow this up and see if I could get into it myself. My first real job was at WLIB in New York, a small station in Harlem that played every kind of music that was important in the black community. The played gospel, jazz, and even classical music performed by African Americans, and that's where it all started."

26 john taylor

Although I'd known John Taylor's work on record, my first experience of hearing him play live was on the massive, magnificent
organ of Salisbury Cathedral during the premiere of John Surman's *Proverbs And Songs*. But as this piece from the December
2001 *Jazzwise* makes clear, Taylor is not only a fine organist, but
one of Britain's most versatile jazz pianists.

One of the downsides of being a jazz critic is that, particularly during the
festival season, concert-going can get a bit numbing. It's all too easy to let
the gigs just wash over you, and it takes something really special or unusual to remind you why it is that you do it, and what it is about the music
that drew you into writing about it in the first place. For that reason, I've
always looked forward to hearing John Taylor in concert. A pianist of brilliant invention and originality, JT, as his colleagues call him, adds lustre
and life to almost any setting, and I've heard him in lots of them, from a
particularly entrancing solo set in Bath's Guildhall to the intimate trio of
Azimuth, and from Kenny Wheeler's quintet or big band to another trio
with Maria Pia de Vito and Ralph Towner. Above all, from all the times
I've heard him in concert, two things stand out most about John for me:
at one extreme his intuitive understanding of the most complex aspects
of John Surman's music, taking in both the long-established quartet and
the church organ in *Proverbs And Songs*, and, at the other, his ability to make
even the most well-worn mainstream numbers sound original, as he did at
Cheltenham's Everyman Theatre with Johnny Griffin, a few years back.

But with the exception of his solo work, and to a lesser extent of Azimuth, in which John is, as it were, the senior partner, he has usually been
part of somebody else's band, or playing someone else's compositions,
rather than leading his own groups to play his own writing. Now that's
about to change, and he'll be starting off the year of his sixtieth birthday
[2002] by going out on the road in a six-concert tour for the Contemporary Music Network leading his own trio and octet. These are not, he was
quick to point out, the same rhythm team adapted to two contexts, but
two entirely separate projects.

John Taylor at the Vortex, London, 2003 (Derek Drescher)

"Each night I'll be doing one set with the trio of Marc Johnson on bass and Joey Baron, drums, and then another set with a group drawn from the Creative Jazz Orchestra. What's unusual about that group is that there's no bass. It'll have me on piano, Martin France on drums, and then Oren Marshall on tuba, plus a French guitarist David Chevalier, whose main reputation rests on his classical playing, but with us he'll be on electric guitar. And the rest of the line-up's reeds and trombone, with Julian Argüelles and Iain Dixon among the saxophones. Some of the music first saw the light of day in 1997 at the Cheltenham Festival, and I hope that part of it'll be out on CD in time for the tour, but now I've written a whole new suite of new pieces called *The Green Man*, with titles loosely based around the places in Britain where there are historical sites connected with green men.

"The trio goes back a bit as well. I first worked with Marc and Joey as the rhythm section on an album for the Dutch trumpeter Eric Vloeimans. But I'd met Joey much, much earlier, over twenty years ago, in the late seventies, when I was with Ronnie Scott's group and Joey came to the club with Betty Carter's trio. I've always liked Joey's playing, and the way he likes to show that there's more to the drums than the military rudiments. One thing that brought his skill home to me was during the sound check for the disc with Eric, when Joey just nonchalantly played the melody of a Monk tune on the drums, instead of the usual stuff drummers do at a sound check. Marc, of course, actually worked with Bill Evans, who was one of my main influences. I particularly like the feeling and the heart in Bill's work, and I feel that I have plenty of connections to that, not just through Marc but also because I've worked from time to time with Bill's former drummer Paul Motian as well."

This sense of a trio that fuses rhythm and melody, and in which the conventional roles of piano, bass and drums are relaxed into a far more democratic interchange of ideas is, of course, at the heart of Azimuth, the trio in which John has played with Norma Winstone and Kenny Wheeler since 1977.

"Back then Norma and I were working together a lot, but I couldn't get anyone to record us. I knew about Manfred Eicher at ECM, and eventually I sent him a demo and then went to talk to him about recording us. During our conversation, Manfred mentioned Kenny, suggesting he might be the 'third member of our duet.' In due course that's what happened, and we ended up recording for ECM. I was delighted by the idea of bringing in Kenny, whom I'd met when he'd turned up as a guest in the late '60s at a pub gig I played in North London with my trio, and we'd been involved in each other's projects quite a bit since then. Back in those days, it wasn't just a question of recording for ECM, there was a lot more to it, and for the first and second Azimuth albums the record company arranged tours for us. It was quite a turning point in our careers, and we began to establish what you might call a collective personality. Nowadays, that's been there for such a long time that the group carries on developing, even though we don't perform as regularly as we once did."

I wondered what kind of development he meant – assuming that John wasn't just talking about the level of musical understanding that goes with such a long period of association.

"Well, for a start, I think the pieces that are built on a text have become more a part of what we do. They've grown because Norma's lyric-writing skill has grown, and because I think we've extended the way we respond collectively to words. Of course there were some complex songs originally, but not as many as we tend to play now. I suppose we've built on the part of our repertoire that includes pieces like *Wintersweet*, which is simply a marvellous tune, a very traditional-sounding ballad by Kenny that has an intimate connection with the words. It's a change that's taken place slowly, over a long period of time, but I'm sure if you compared a gig from the '70s with a more recent one, that would be the main difference."

John's collaboration with John Surman has matured over a similar time-frame. They first worked together in the 1960s in Surman's octet, and then recorded the following decade on Surman's *Morning Glory* album with guitarist Terje Rypdal. But it wasn't until 1993 that Surman's quartet produced its masterpiece, *Stranger Than Fiction*.

"We've grown up both together and apart," said John. "All the stuff each of us does outside feeds back in, and we reinvent ourselves as a group each time we get together, which is usually around every six months or so. Surman always wanted this to be principally an improvising group, and I think we've managed to retain that. Obviously when we get together we play some of the same repertoire, but always in a very fresh way. I think it helped that our second disc for ECM was done quite late in the day, and we had a chance to encapsulate a lot of what hadn't been caught on record during the previous twenty years or so. But certainly we get on really well, and I think that comes across on the disc."

One reason that much of Taylor's work seems to have developed in a somewhat stop-start fashion is that for the last ten years he's been a tutor at the music academy in Cologne. "It's a permanent half-time position," he said. "I started there when I was fifty, and I'd never had a job like that before, but I have to organize my time extremely carefully, and build my other travels around these regular trips to Germany. The biggest problem is finding time to write my own music, but in a way it's been very helpful to have a teaching job on the continent because, frankly, I do most of my playing in Europe because there just isn't enough work in the UK."

Like many others who have a foot in the education world, John has formed firm friendships and associations with his colleagues in Cologne, and British audiences will have the chance to see one of these in action in May 2002 at the Bath International Music Festival, when he'll be appearing with the former WDR big band trombonist Henning Berg. "He and I will be playing in something called Tango and Company, with clarinettist Gabriele Mirabassi. But it's not to do with tango dancing. It's the name of some computer software that Henning has developed that is actually an improvisation programme. As far as I know it's one of the first attempts at interactive computer improvisation, and although what the machine produces is dependent on what we play it does create a genuinely new improvisation from it. So that'll be an interesting experiment to bring to Britain."

As well as this appearance and his own Contemporary Music Network tour, 2002 will also find John in a new collaboration on disc with Maria Pia de Vito and Ralph Towner, plus Steve Swallow on bass. That will be recorded just before his tour, and at the same time he is writing new music both for his trio with Marc Johnson and Joey Baron, and for a major solo concert in Cologne. Having had a year-long bursary for composition, John found time to write the *Green Man* suite, and he's itching to find more time to continue as a composer. "As I said, I don't get enough time to write, but having brought out a lot of my old music for a one-off big band at the Vortex club in London eighteen months ago, and then going on to produce *Green Man*, it's spurred my interest in writing for smaller forces. I'm certainly going to be finding time to write more for solo piano, and the Cologne concert has given me the spur to compose for my own instrument, rather than for a band or even a trio."

27 butch thompson

I have known Butch Thompson for almost as long as I've been listening to or playing jazz seriously. We met in the mid-1970s during one of my earliest visits to New Orleans, and since then I have played with him in a variety of contexts, but most pleasurably and memorably in the "King Oliver Centennial Band" which Butch assembled to commemorate Joe "King" Oliver's one-hundredth birthday at the 1985 Ascona Festival in Switzerland. That year, and on a number of subsequent annual tours, Butch proved that it is possible to tackle much of Oliver's repertoire in the manner of the Creole Jazz Band, without slavish copying, but with a degree of affectionate respect. Since then, we have played together in the New Orleans Serenaders, both in Europe and the United States, and Butch has collaborated with me on a BBC series about the craft of Harlem "stride" piano. This interview is from the October 2003 edition of *Piano*.

The compositions of Jelly Roll Morton make up one of the largest collections of early jazz music by any single composer or songwriter. From the first tunes he copyrighted in 1915, such as *Jelly Roll Blues* up to his 1930s numbers such as *Sweet Peter*, Morton developed ragtime ideas into jazz, with a particular sense of time and swing. A small number of pianists round the world specialize in interpreting his music, and foremost among them is Butch Thompson, from Minnesota. In July 2003, while Butch was appearing at the Ascona Festival of New Orleans Jazz in Switzerland, we spoke about his fascination for Morton and his contemporaries.

"I first heard the solo piano recordings from 1923 and 1924 when I was eighteen or so, and for some reason they connected with me immediately," Butch recalled. "I had never heard anything quite like them and I knew instantly this was something I wanted to do myself. Earlier I had been trying to play boogie woogie, and I'd been working out pieces by Jimmy Yancey and Albert Ammons. I also liked the playing of Teddy Wilson, whom I'd heard on my father's collection of discs. But Morton's music really hit me in a different way, and the more I worked on it the

Butch Thompson in his other guise as a clarinettist. The other musicians (l–r) are Richard Simmons, piano; Alyn Shipton, bass; Jim Holmes, trumpet; and Dave Evans, drums (Author's collection)

more I realized both how much there was to learn, and how impossible it was to figure everything out, especially from acoustic recordings like those, which were not in the best quality to start with.

"I kept trying, and my initial way of working was just to listen and listen, copying what I heard. I didn't realize at the time that there were enthusiasts who had made transcriptions of the solos, some of which had been published in the 1940s by Morton's friend Roy Carew and his company Tempo Music. Other collectors had transcriptions that had not been published, including the New Orleans-based record producer Bill Russell, who had a vast collection. Around 1962, I met Bill, while I was still working on learning this music by ear, and didn't know until a couple of years afterwards that he had all these things. But he became a big help to me later, by introducing me to the written music.

"J. Lawrence Cook, whom Carew got to do the transcriptions for Tempo Music, was really something of a genius because he figured out completely what Morton's voicings were, and how the effects were achieved on the piano. He had Morton's compositional system worked out, by which I mean he could convey the polyphonic music you might hear from an early jazz band by using particular configurations for the right hand. Morton's talent was to suggest the notes, without making it necessary to play all the parts in every single line. It was a hard thing to do in the first place, and equally hard for Cook to capture by ear from those old recordings, but there were certain tricks involved which I was really able to learn once I studied the Cook transcriptions. There were something like a couple of dozen of them altogether, although not all of them were published.

"The same elements are there in the music which was published from Morton's original handwritten versions. The *Original Jelly Roll Blues*, for example, from 1915, although it had an extra vocal line added for a singer, sounds just like Morton playing the piano in terms of its voicings and chord structure.

"Once I'd got all this figured out, it actually took me a while to get out of Morton's thrall, and start exploring other things because for years I tried to play everything exactly like Jelly Roll Morton. I applied his style to all manner of tunes, from Broadway show songs to Dixieland numbers, wondering 'How would Jelly Roll do this?'

"I was also quite successful in performing this music in public, for example at the St Louis ragtime festival in 1968, where they didn't have any other Morton specialists at the time, although they did have many other fine pianists including Eubie Blake and Dick Wellstood. That year was the Scott Joplin centennial, so all these famous pianists were there, and I was very much the New Orleans specialist, not least because I was also becoming known as a traditional clarinet player, and I had immersed myself in that aspect of New Orleans music. It wasn't really until the great Joplin revival of the 1970s, in the wake of *The Sting*, that I branched out into other areas of jazz and ragtime piano myself. After all in the mid-70s if you didn't play *The Entertainer* you didn't get a lot of work!

"So I began to really study Joplin's writing in the 1970s. And that led me to discover other things because I had respected James P. Johnson, Fats Waller, Willie 'The Lion' Smith and the other stride players from a distance, and now I realized there was a lot to be learned from them.

"One possible problem in incorporating their work into my style was that Morton had a very distinct concept of time, and his idea of what you might call swing was very different from Fats and the New York guys. But there was one pianist who really managed a synthesis of Morton's style and stride playing, and that was the late Don Ewell. You could identify all his influences, but he really played like himself, even if you heard the odd Morton right-hand voicing offset by a Fats Waller stride pattern in his left hand, and he drew together this entire tradition into something of his own. In due course achieving that kind of synthesis became something I worked on too, and today I'm now more than ever convinced that it can be done."

28 sir charles thompson

When I was working with New Orleans guitarist Danny Barker on the first volume of his memoirs, he produced a pile of photographs to be considered for inclusion. One of his favourites, which appears in the finished book, *A Life In Jazz*, is of Sir Charles Thompson's band, recording for Aladdin with Charlie Parker, Buck Clayton and Dexter Gordon. At the back sits Danny, with his hat on, as was often the fashion in those far-off days.

Danny and I talked about the session, and I hoped that one day I would meet Sir Charles and find out more about the man who led the band. My appetite was further whetted by hearing the marvellous recordings Sir Charles made with Buck Clayton's All Stars on tour in Europe, and then by seeing him play in a BBC film of Coleman Hawkins's touring band, with Sweets Edison, Jimmy Woode and Jo Jones. So I felt very fortunate to have the chance to visit him in California while researching a tribute series for BBC Radio about Miles Davis. Once we had recorded our material for the radio, we sat back in Sir Charles's sunny apartment, and continued to talk. The results appeared in the January 2002 edition of *Piano*.

One of the legendary figures in jazz piano, Sir Charles Thompson is looking forward to his eighty-fourth birthday in March 2002. Despite reaching an age when many musicians have long-since retired, he's still playing regularly, and has just released his latest album, recorded live at Joe Segal's Jazz Showcase in Chicago in summer 2001. His style is instantly recognizable – particularly his single-line right-hand solos, which are pared away to the most spartan of statements, but which are delivered with a rhythmic precision that makes even Count Basie's economical style sound cluttered.

When he's not on the road, Sir Charles can be found living quietly in his home at the foot of the Hollywood hills, or indulging in his lifelong passion for golf. Indeed, when I met him, he launched into an enthusiastic explanation of the similarities between playing jazz piano and being a good golfer, ranging from practice regimes to the need for improvisation – both, as he said with a chuckle, "don't mean a thing if they ain't got that swing."

He sees himself as an all-round pianist, able to fit into any style of jazz, from the big band arrangements he began playing as a teenager in the Territories of the Midwest, to the swing styles he mastered in the groups of Lester Young and Coleman Hawkins, and on to the modern jazz which he played night after night on New York's 52nd Street with Charlie Parker and Miles Davis. He is also a composer of some note, having written the standard *Robbins' Nest* while he was a member of the band led by tenorist Illinois Jacquet, and he's proud of his achievements as a bandleader, particularly some of the earliest discs that feature Charlie Parker and Dexter Gordon, with the All Star studio band he led in 1945.

His nickname "Sir" Charles came from the early 1940s, when he was working with Lester Young at the Café Society in Greenwich Village in New York, where Young so liked his playing that he pronounced, "You need one of those fancy names like Duke Ellington or Count Basie, so I'm gonna call you 'Sir' Charles." He did, and the name stuck. Thompson says he still feels it an honour to have had the name bestowed on him by one

Sir Charles Thompson in London during his 1967 tour with Coleman Hawkins
(Mike Doyle/Symil)

of his own musical heroes. And, in particular, a hero who had played in the band led by Thompson's greatest inspiration of all, Count Basie.

The Count's influence on him goes back to his childhood, growing up as the son of a Methodist minister in Colorado Springs. Sir Charles was just ten years old when Basie's band came to town to play for a local dance, where having being told by some friends that the youngster played piano, Basie persuaded Thompson to come up on stage and play for the band's intermission. His friendliness and encouragement made a deep impression on the young boy, and Sir Charles continues to look up to Basie to this day as the man who really got him started in music.

It was another member of Basie's own band, trumpeter Buck Clayton, who urged the teenage Sir Charles to turn professional. Clayton's father was also a Methodist minister, and at one point worked alongside Thompson's father in the Clayton family's home town of Parsons, Kansas. And it was there, at a neighbourhood jam session at the house of organist Wild Bill Davis, that Sir Charles ended up accompanying Buck, at the same time cementing a lifelong friendship and being urged by the trumpeter to go out on the road in his own right.

Before long Sir Charles was working with another trumpeter in Omaha, Nebraska, called Lloyd Hunter, and soon afterwards he joined the legendary band of Nat Towles, a bassist who led what is widely regarded by jazz historians as the finest Territory band never to make any records. "I became the pianist and arranger for the Nat Towles Orchestra. Nat was a very smart businessman, and he led one of the best bands in the Midwest, but he didn't have time for anyone who wasn't going to pay him properly. It was the same type of band as Basie's, but I think it was the money, or the lack of it, that stopped us from making any discs. Nat just didn't get offered what he thought was a fair price."

Also in the group were saxophonist Buddy Tate and trombonist Henry Coker, both of whom went on to join Basie's orchestra in due course. But as young men, they criss-crossed the small towns of the Midwest, playing barn dances, theatres and town halls, often meeting other bands who were out on the same circuit between St Louis, Kansas City and Omaha, such as Jay McShann's Orchestra with the young Charlie Parker among his saxophonists. Thompson is one of the very few musicians who worked with Parker in later life who heard him in those early days, and who confirmed to me that, "he had his conception of music in place at that time, but he hadn't quite pulled it all together. His new ideas didn't make sense to us then. Nobody, including me (and I became a good friend of his) understood it. And not many bandleaders, apart from McShann, would have wanted somebody playing like that in their band.

But later on he perfected it, and it became the basis of the bebop style that changed the whole face of jazz."

So how had Sir Charles made the transition to playing this style himself when he eventually came to New York?

"I think that comes from being a congenial accompanist and trying to play the right chords for a soloist. I had the good fortune of knowing chords and harmony pretty well, having been an arranger, and that's how I ended up playing with Bird on 52nd Street in the mid-'40s. I also played uptown a lot at Minton's Playhouse, where Thelonious Monk was the regular pianist. I'd got to New York by way of California because in 1939 a West Coast bandleader called Floyd Ray came through Omaha, heard me play, and asked me to join his band. I went out to California with him. While I was there I met Lionel Hampton, around the time he left Benny Goodman, and I joined Lionel's first big band. It came back to the East Coast in 1940, and I ended up in New York.

"Lionel got the best musicians he could find from all over the United States. There was saxophonist Marshal Royal, who was a genius musician and a well-schooled disciplinarian, who trained the sax section, which included Dexter Gordon and Illinois Jacquet. Of course they were heavily into some of the more modern ideas in jazz, and so was our guitarist Irving Ashby, who played like Charlie Christian. It was a fantastic band, and one of the most exciting times in my life."

I wondered if it was while they worked together with Lionel Hampton that Sir Charles and Illinois Jacquet had collaborated on writing *Robbins' Nest*.

"No. That was a few years later, when we were both living back out here in California. Illinois had made his name by that time, with Cab Calloway, Basie and Lionel Hampton, and of course he'd recorded his famous solos for Jazz At The Philharmonic. I'd played on some of those concerts too, but he was the one who really became famous because of his *Blues Part 2*. He had a record date in 1947, and it hadn't gone particularly well. We had no more than five minutes of studio time left, and he asked me if I'd got any tunes up my sleeve that we could play. I said yes, and just roughed out for him on the piano the introduction and the first theme. I told him we'd play that together, do a little question and answer routine, and then I said, you take a couple of solo choruses and then we'll play the piece out. So we did it, and in less than five minutes we'd created a hit, but it is just a very simple idea, and that's one of the principles of my musical life, to be clear and simple."

It seemed strange that a musician who's so keen on simplicity and elegant, unadorned melody lines should have been so close to Charlie

Parker, whose music seems the very opposite. But Sir Charles was quick to point out that Parker's complexity always had a simple underlying beat and it was close to the blues.

"When I got the chance to make the first records of my own, for the Apollo label, I naturally asked all my friends from the last few years to come and join in. So that's why I had Charlie Parker, Dexter Gordon and Buck Clayton, three musicians who I'd always be happy to play with, even for nothing in a jam session. Buck was still in the army, but it was very fortunate that he was around in New York when I had the record date. He played the session in uniform. Later on he repaid the compliment, and he was the first musician to bring me to Europe in his band a few years later. That was another of the great thrills of my life, to cross the Atlantic and come face to face with so many European jazz fans."

In our afternoon of conversation, Sir Charles brought up several other moments that had been equally exciting for him, but one that really stood out was working as Billie Holiday's accompanist. "That was a really humbling experience. She could be really temperamental, but the other side of the coin was that she could also be very courteous and nice. She knew that I was a young pianist and didn't know all her songs, but she had a way about her of creating a pure jazz performance out of anything she sang that would make anyone feel good, so I was relieved that the temperamental side of her didn't come out!"

For many jazz critics, myself included, Sir Charles has seldom surpassed his playing on the Septet recordings he made with Vic Dickenson in 1953–54. He laughed warmly at the memory, and said, "For me, apart from my own discs with Charlie Parker and Dexter, the sessions with Vic were the most enjoyable to play on of my whole career. This was mainly because Vic was such a wonderful person. He was also from Ohio, where I was actually born, and his personality was very warm and very encouraging. He said very little to us in the studio, just created the right atmosphere for us to play. And the results were fantastic; to me that is jazz at its best, with Edmond Hall on clarinet, Ruby Braff on cornet, bringing the music they'd made together in Boston to a wider audience. I'd lived in Boston for a while, playing with Ruby and Ed, and I think that long experience of working together shows, too."

And jumping forward to the present day, Sir Charles is one of the most experienced pianists still recording. His relaxed solos with just bass and drums accompaniment, or his quartet numbers with tenorist Eric Schneider from his new album, *I Got Rhythm, Live At The Jazz Showcase*, just go to show that he is still able to create jazz at its best.

29 mal waldron

One of the least pleasant duties of a regular columnist is to record the passing of significant musicians. This tribute to Mal Waldron, based on one of the last interviews he gave before his death, was published by *Piano* in March 2003.

Although there had been rumours that he was suffering from a serious illness for some time, the death of jazz pianist Mal Waldron from cancer in December 2002 was a shock to his many friends and fans around the world, and particularly in Europe, where he settled in the 1960s. In recent years, he had been a frequent visitor to Britain, travelling from his home in Belgium to play and compose for the Oxfordshire-based saxophonist George Haslam. And it was on one of those trips that Mal and I met in the quiet surroundings of Abingdon, to reflect on a roller-coaster career in jazz during which he recorded with everyone from Charles Mingus to Billie Holiday. But we began by talking about his move to Paris, in 1963.

"I like to think of that as my second life," he said slowly, with an ironic grin, as he fiddled with his ever-present cigarette. "Because I had already died once before I left America. I took an overdose of drugs, and I was clinically dead for a few minutes. When I came to, I couldn't remember anything. I didn't know who I was, my name, or anything. I couldn't remember any music – no chord changes, no tunes, nothing. And my hands were trembling so much I couldn't play the piano. Then I was moved to another hospital where they gave me spinal taps and electric shock treatment – a whole range of things designed to take the pressure off my brain. It took about a year before I was well enough to return to music, and even longer to be able to play changes and to improvise. Although I learned how to play again, which I did partly by listening to my own records, I couldn't really improvise any more because I couldn't think fast enough, so for almost the next two years, I worked out my solos in advance and played what I had written out, until gradually all my faculties returned."

I suggested that it must have been very tough for him to stick to such a formidable process of rehabilitation, but he disagreed. "Music, for me,

Mal Waldron during a BBC "Impressions" recording, Maida Vale Studios, 1994
(Derek Drescher)

was always like breathing. If you don't breathe, you die, so having come back to life, for me it wasn't a choice, I just had to do it, but I noticed enormous changes in the way I played. Before I collapsed, I was a very lyrical player, but I couldn't find that lyricism inside myself any more, so I became a very angular player."

I suggested that this didn't just apply to his playing but to his composition because instead of delicate ballads like his most famous composition *Soul Eyes*, written in 1957, he created chunky, angular pieces such as the blues tune *Spaces* which he included on a recent album, and which seems to have its melody line hewn out of breeze blocks.

"Yes," he agreed, "I became closer to the way Thelonious Monk played and wrote than I was before. I guess if you think in terms of my fellow bebop players, before 1963 I was more like Bud Powell, although ironically I only got to know Bud well after I moved to Paris, when he was also there for a while, and by then I couldn't play in his style any longer."

One thing Mal began to specialize in after settling in Europe was playing duos, and he has recorded many of them, with American saxophonists Steve Lacy and Jim Pepper, with George Haslam here in Britain, and most recently, on the posthumously released *Riding A Zephyr*, with singer Judy Silvano. I wondered if he'd chosen this format for economic or artistic reasons.

"A bit of both, but mainly artistic. I think jazz is really a conversation. It's a language, and you communicate with other musicians. So to do this face to face, it is more direct, stronger and more accurate. If you have to speak to two or three people at the same time, then it becomes a little more diffuse, so I love the clarity of duo playing, and the ability to respond instantaneously."

I suggested that this linked back to his earlier work in the United States, when he was regarded as one of the most sublime accompanists in jazz, particularly during the two years he spent with Billie Holiday from 1957 until her death in 1959. Many commentators regard this late period in her life, when she was herself ravaged by drugs and hard living, as a tragic decline, but Mal didn't see it that way at all. "She was very happy at that time, very funny, told jokes, saw humour in everything. Although her voice was not as it had been before, she adapted brilliantly to what she had left to work with."

At the same time as he was working in clubs and concerts with Holiday, Mal was recording prolifically as the house pianist for Prestige records. "I was often asked to write original music for the sessions," he recalled. "It might be as many as six or eight tunes, sometimes working overnight, so we could record them in the studio the next day. They'd tell me who was going to be on the session, and I'd write material that I thought was suitable in terms of their playing style. I was first introduced to Prestige by the altoist Jackie McLean, and they liked me because I was dependable and I also knew how to write. So it began to snowball, and I ended up playing on dozens of sessions. I think John Coltrane was one of the most memorable. He was very focused, practising all the time he was off stage. I used to play gigs with him at the Five Spot in New York, and when we went back to the kitchen to relax during our break, he'd be standing in a corner trying out new runs, new figures, to play during the next set. I could never do that; even before I collapsed, I liked to relax, hang out, enjoy myself when I wasn't actually playing."

30 gerald wiggins

The final piece in this collection appeared in *Piano* in March 2002. Although Gerald Wiggins is well-known in Los Angeles, and among jazz record collectors, he deserves to be far better known by the public at large. His playing crosses many stylistic boundaries, and his work has consistently shown him to be in the very highest echelon of solo players.

In pride of place in Gerald Wiggins's music room is a huge signed portrait of Marilyn Monroe, looking directly across his piano to where he sits at the keyboard. He looked up at it and grinned.

"Oh yes! Marilyn," he said. "I met her through the drummer in my trio, Jackie Mills, who'd been playing in various backing groups for her. And from then on, for every movie in which she sang, I coached her for the vocals. Her style was to kind of speak the words, almost in a whisper, and then just sing the occasional phrase. And under my tuition, she became a pretty fast learner. I used to teach her a little riff to sing here and there, and when she got to the studio the band arrangers there would jump right on it, and put it in the score for the soundtrack. I never got any credit for that, but when she gave me that photo it was a 'thank you' for all those movies we worked on together."

Today, as he has been for over fifty years, Gerald Wiggins, known universally in Los Angeles as "Wig," is the doyen of West Coast jazz pianists. Friend of such luminaries as Nat King Cole and Art Tatum, he has led a trio consistently since the late 1940s, and his playing encompasses all the harmonic and rhythmic developments that followed bebop, without ever sacrificing a natural sense of swing, or what his fellow pianist Jimmy Rowles called his "natural relaxation." He has matured gently with time and on his latest discs from the 1990s, including his solo contribution to the Maybeck Recital Hall series, his playing is better than ever.

I was in Los Angeles to research a radio series on the city's lost jazz scene on Central Avenue, which was a thriving jazz centre until it gradually faded away in the 1950s, and its dozens of clubs closed. I sought out Wig because he played in most of them, including a lengthy residency at the Turban Room, a long, low saloon next door to the Dunbar Hotel, which is now a landmark and almost the only surviving building from that heyday of West Coast jazz. But when he arrived in L.A., Wig was far from the celebrated figure he is now.

"The local musicians hated me with a vengeance because I was a New Yorker," he told me. "I'd come out here with Les Hite's band, one of the best Californian swing orchestras, which I joined on the same day

Gerald Wiggins (Concord Records)

as Dizzy Gillespie, back in the East. I had been on the same bill as Les at a theatre in Brooklyn, when I was backing up the old-time comedian, Stepin Fetchit. He got in some trouble with the police and had to pull out of his act, and the same day Les's piano player got called into the army because this was 1942. So I took the piano job with Les, and I was amazed when I showed up for rehearsal to find Dizzy in the band as well. I knew him well from one of those New York after-hours clubs where bebop was developing, Monroe's Uptown House because I'd been house piano player there when Dizzy came to try out all his new numbers. I had been playing there for just $3 a night, but I was still in my teens and it was a job playing jazz, which was what I wanted.

"Les Hite was a nice man, and when the band played he'd come out in front of us and shake some maracas. Well, behind his back, Dizzy would stand up and mimic him. He kept the whole band and the audience in stitches. Of course, every time Les turned round, Dizzy would be sitting back in his chair as if nothing had happened. But, of course, Les knew what was going on, and he began to get worried because not long before that, when Dizzy was in Cab Calloway's band, there had been an altercation, and Dizzy cut Cab with a knife. Les didn't want that happening to him, so he fired the whole band, and then hired us back again one by one, so he could get rid of Dizzy! Before he went, we made some great records, including *Jersey Bounce*, where you can hear Diz's new solo ideas over our rhythm section, which had a great drummer, Oscar Bradley, and guitarist Frank Pasley. We tried to get the same kind of lift in our playing as the Basie band. Anyhow, I travelled with Les Hite to California, and I remember the day we arrived in Los Angeles, it was Christmas Day, and the temperature was 100 degrees. I told myself this is where I want to stay!"

And stay he did, initially joining the band led by another expatriate New Yorker, Benny Carter, until he won the acceptance from the locals, and began working with saxophonist Buddy Collette and drummer Chico Hamilton. From there he found plenty of work in the studios, right through the era when every studio had its own permanent roster of musicians on salary, whether they worked or not. But from shortly after his.arrival, Wig always led his own trio, playing his own very special brand of jazz. Perhaps it is the relaxed atmosphere of Los Angeles, perhaps it is his own laid-back temperament, but Wig can make even the most frantic tempo sound unhurried, with space to develop solo lines that have interior light and shade, however rapid – a good example being his famous composition *Da Silva Wig*, which is on the Rhino Records compilation of Central Avenue Sounds.

And maybe, it occurred to me afterwards as I was driving back to downtown Los Angeles from Wig's peaceful house in the hills above the city, it was that very feeling of relaxation that made him such a successful voice coach. It wasn't just Marilyn Monroe who benefited from Wig's unhurried accompaniments – and later he modestly listed for me the singers he's worked with, including Lena Horne, Dinah Washington, Dinah Shore and Kay Starr. All of whom, I suspect, were as charmed by his unassuming nature and keyboard brilliance, as I was.

selected recordings

This is by no means an exhaustive list, but in most cases points towards discs directly related to the conversations, or provides background and context to them. So, for example, I have not listed all the Keith Jarrett ECM catalogue, but I have listed the majority of his work with the Standards Trio. In his case and that of Carla Bley their output is well represented by the :Rarum Selected Recordings anthologies on ECM. Wider-ranging conversations, such as those with Herbie Hancock or Chick Corea, have been followed up here with more general surveys of their output.

Carla Bley
Escalator Over The Hill (JCOA/ECM) 1968-71
Live! (Watt) 1981
The Very Big Carla Bley Band (Watt) 1990
Goes To Church (Watt) 1996
Are We There Yet? (with Steve Swallow) (Watt) 1999
4x4 (Watt) 1999
Looking For America (Watt) 2003
Carla Bley also appears on *Gary Burton: A Genuine Tong Funeral* (RCA) 1967–68

JoAnne Brackeen
Pink Elephant Magic (Arkadia) 1998
Popsicle Illusion (Arkadia) 1999
Quartet At The Jazz Standard (Arkadia) 2003

Dave Brubeck
40th Anniversary Tour Of The UK (Telarc) 1998
The Crossing (Telarc) 2000
One Alone (Telarc) 2000
80th Birthday Concert (LSO Live) 2000

Uri Caine

Urlicht (Winter and Winter) 1996
Goldberg (Winter and Winter) 2000
Solitaire (Winter and Winter) 2001
Bedrock 3 (Winter and Winter) 2001
Rio (Winter and Winter) 2001

Alice Coltrane

Eternity (Warner) 1976
Transcendence (Warner) 1976
Transfiguration (Warner) 1976
Rada-Krsna Nama Sankirtana (Warner) 1977

Chick Corea

Music Forever And Beyond (GRP) 1964–96
Tones For Joan's Bones (Atlantic) 1966
A.R.C. (ECM) 1971
Return To Forever (ECM) 1972
Crystal Silence (with Gary Burton) (ECM) 1979
Akoustic Band (GRP) 1979
Origin: Live At The Blue Note (Stretch) 1998
Past, Present And Futures (Stretch) 2001

Sylvie Courvoisier

Abaton (ECM) 2003

Tommy Flanagan

At The Village Vanguard (Blue Note) 1998

Michael Garrick

Rendell-Carr Quintet: Phase III / Live (BGO) 1967–68
Rendell-Carr Quintet: Change Is (BGO) 1969
Troppo (Argo) 1974
Meteors Close At Hand (Jaza) 1994
New Quartet (Jaza) 2001
Green and Pleasant Land (Jaza) 2002
Peter Pan Jazz Dance Suite (Jaza) 2003

Benny Green

Lineage (Blue Note) 1990
Testifyin' – Live At The Village Vanguard (Blue Note) 1991
That's Right! (Blue Note) 1992

Oscar And Benny (with Oscar Peterson) (Telarc) 1998
Naturally (Telarc) 2000
Green's Blues (Telarc) 2001

Herbie Hancock

Takin' Off (Blue Note) 1962
Empyrean Isles (Blue Note) 1964
Maiden Voyage (Blue Note) 1965
Speak Like A Child (Blue Note) 1968
The Prisoner (Blue Note) 1969
Fat Albert Rotunda (Warner Bros) 1969
Mwandishi (Warner Bros) 1970
Sextant (Warner Bros) 1972
Head Hunters (Columbia) 1973
V.S.O.P. (Columbia) 1976
An Evening With Herbie Hancock And Chick Corea (Columbia) 1978
Future Shock (Columbia) 1983
The New Standard (Verve) 1996
Gershwin's World (Verve) 1998
Future 2 Future (Transparent) 2001

Andrew Hill

Judgement (Blue Note) 1964
Point Of Departure (Blue Note) 1964
Verona Rag (Soul Note) 1986
Eternal Spirit (Blue Note) 1989
But Not Farewell (Blue Note) 1990
Dusk (Palmetto) 2000

Abdullah Ibrahim

Sathima Bea Benjamin: *A Morning In Paris* (Enja) 1963
African Marketplace (Discovery) 1979
The Mountain (Camden) 1985
Desert Flowers (Enja) 1991
Cape Town Revisited (Enja/Tiptoe) 1997

Keith Jarrett

Standards Vols 1 and 2 (ECM) 1983
Standards Live (ECM) 1985
At The Blue Note: Complete Recordings (ECM) 1994
Tokyo '96 (ECM) 1996

Whisper Not (ECM) 1999
Inside Out (ECM) 2000
Always Let Me Go (ECM) 2001
Up For It (ECM) 2003

Brian Kellock

Something's Got To Give (Caber) 1998
The Crossing (with Tam White) (Caber) 2000
Live At Henry's (Caber) 2000
John Rae's Celtic Feet: Beware The Feet (Caber) 2001

Diana Krall

Stepping Out (Justin Time) 1993
All For You (Impulse) 1995
Love Scenes (Impulse) 1997
When I Look In Your Eyes (Verve) 1997
The Look Of Love (Verve) 1997
The Girl In The Other Room (Verve) 2004

John Lewis

Bach's Forty-eight (Philips) 1984
The Private Concert (Emarcy) 1990
Evolution (Atlantic/Warner Jazz) 1999

Jacques Loussier

Plays Bach (Telarc) 1993
Vivaldi: The Four Seasons (Telarc) 1997
Erik Satie: Gymnopédies/Gnossiennes (Telarc) 1998
Ravels' Bolero (Telarc) 1999
Plays Debussy (Telarc) 2000
Bach's Goldberg Variations (Telarc) 2000
Music of Handel (Telarc) 2002

Junior Mance

Live At The Village Vanguard (Original Jazz Classics) 1961
Junior Mance Special (Sackville) 1988
Softly As In A Morning Sunrise (Enja) 1994

Marian McPartland

Jimmy McPartland: *Goin' Back A Ways* (Halcyon) 1948–49 (LP)
On 52nd Street (Savoy) 1953

Personal Choice (Concord) 1982
Live At Maybeck Recital Hall (Concord) 1991
Plays The Music Of Mary Lou Williams (Concord) 1998
Just Friends (Concord) 1998
Hickory House Trio – Reprise (Concord) 1998
Live At Shanghai Jazz (Concord) 2002

Oscar Peterson

1951 (Just A Memory) 1951
At Zardi's (Pablo) 1955
Live At CBC Studios (Just A Memory) 1961
Sound Of The Trio (Verve) 1961
Girl Talk (MPS) 1964–66
The Trio (Original Jazz Classics) 1973
Live At The Blue Note (Telarc) 1990
A Summer Night In Munich (Telarc) 1999
The Very Tall Band – Live At The Blue Note (Telarc) 1998
A Jazz Odyssey (Verve) 2002 (anthology of older material)

Michel Petrucciani

Pianism (Blue Note) 1985
Au Théâtre Des Champs-Elysées (Dreyfus) 1994
Solo Love (Dreyfus) 1997
Conversation (Dreyfus) 1992 (issued 2001)

Horace Silver

Retrospective (Blue Note) 1952-78
Stan Getz: The Roost Quartets (Roulette) 1950–51
Prescription For The Blues (Impulse) 1997
Jazz Has A Sense Of Humor (Verve) 1998

Esbjörn Svensson

Trio Plays Monk (ACT) 1996
Winter In Venice (ACT) 1997
From Gagarin's Point Of View (ACT) 1998
Good Morning Susie Soho (ACT) 2000
Strange Place For Snow (ACT) 2001
Seven Days Of Falling (ACT) 2003

Billy Taylor

Billy Taylor Trio (Prestige) 1952–53
Cross Section (Prestige) 1953–54

Wish I Knew How It Would Feel To Be Free (Tower) 1967
Music Keeps Us Young (Arkadia) 1996

John Taylor
Azimuth/Touchstone/Départ (ECM) 1977–79
Azimuth '85 (ECM) 1985
Blue Glass (Ronnie Scott's Jazz House) 1991
Maria Pia De Vito: *Nel Respiro* (Provocateur) 2002
Rosslyn (ECM) 2003

Butch Thompson
Plays Jelly Roll Morton (Biograph) 1968
A Solas (Stomp Off) 1982
King Oliver Centennial Band (GHB) 1988
Chicago Breakdown (Daring) 1989
Good Old New York (Daring) 1989
New Orleans Joys (Daring) 1989
Plays Joplin (Daring) 1997

Sir Charles Thompson
Takin' Off (Delmark) 1945–47
Vic Dickenson: *The Essential Vic Dickenson* (Vanguard) 1953–54
Charlie Parker: *At Storyville* (Blue Note) 1953
Hey There (Black and Blue) 1974
Live At The Jazz Showcase (Delmark) 2000
I Got Rhythm (Delmark) 2001

Mal Waldron
Mal: Vols 1–4 (Original Jazz Classics) 1956–58
Free At Last (ECM) 1969
Blues For Lady Day (Black Lion) 1972
Soul Eyes (RCA) 1996
Ridin' A Zephyr (with Judy Silvano) (High Note) 2002

Gerald Wiggins
Gerald Wiggins Trio (Discovery) 1953
Reminiscin' With Wig (Motif) 1957
Relax And Enjoy It (Discovery) 1961
Live At Maybeck Vol. 8 (Concord) 1990
Soulidarity (Concord) 1995

index

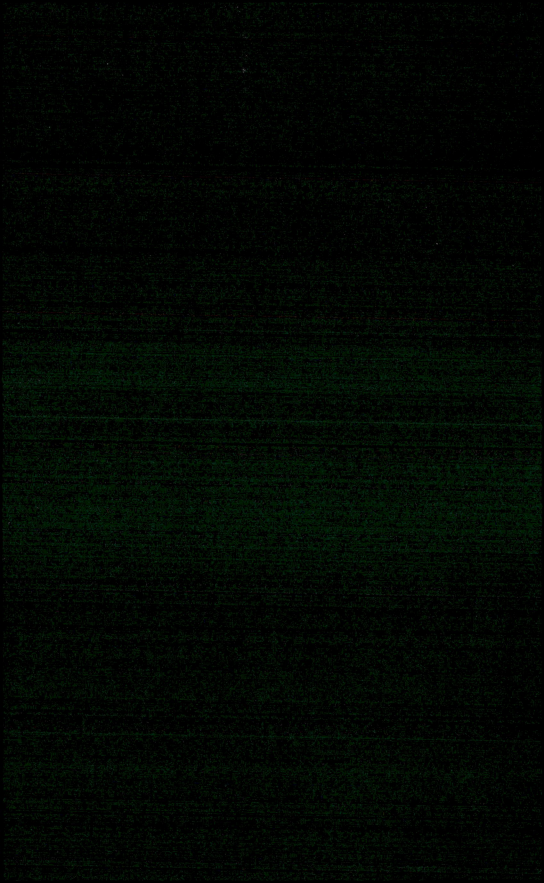